PAST & PRESENT

RIPON

This billboard was part of the United States Tire Company's advertising campaign in the 1920s. In that era, companies were taking advantage of the fact that cars were on the road and tires were always needed. The company was established in 1892, and it later became Uniroyal. (Author's collection.)

On the Cover: Irvin Almont Goodwin came to Ripon in 1907. He started in business with a blacksmith shop on Main Street, as shown in the photograph. It later expanded to a garage and mechanic's shop. When the fire department was first beginning, Goodwin constructed their first apparatus. He was very involved in the community. When Ripon decided it needed a board of trade prior to having a chamber of commerce, Goodwin was one of the principals in that group. It is incredible how a simple business can make such a difference. (Author's collection.)

PAST & PRESENT

RIPON

John P. Mangelos

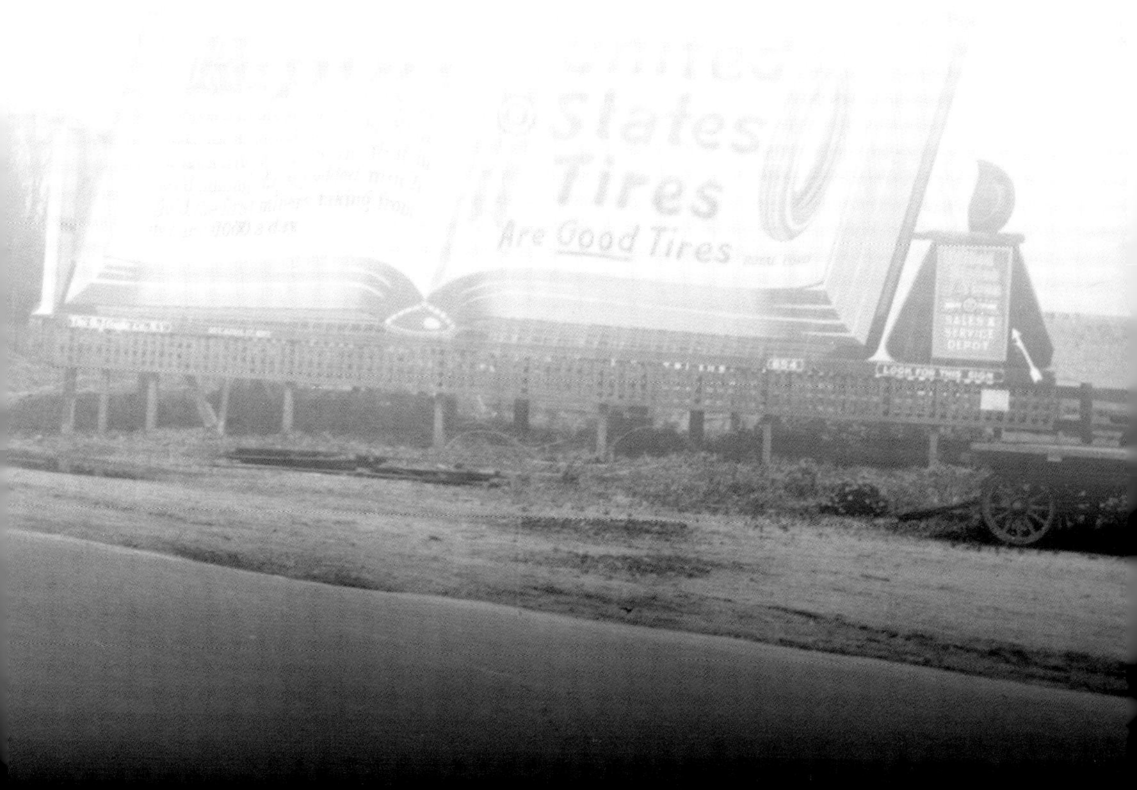

ISBN 978-1-4671-0610-8

Library of Congress Control Number: 2020946945

Published by Arcadia Publishing
Charleston, South Carolina

Printed in the United States of America

For all general information, please contact Arcadia Publishing:
Telephone 843-853-2070
Fax 843-853-0044
E-mail sales@arcadiapublishing.com
For customer service and orders:
Toll-Free 1-888-313-2665

Visit us on the Internet at www.arcadiapublishing.com

Contents

Acknowledgments

When putting a book together, one realizes it is more than just words and photographs on the page. We want to make sure that we tell the story correctly and as concisely as we can. In doing this, we often turn to our family for assistance, hoping the words that we put on the page will send the message that we are trying to say. This project was no different. I am fortunate that my sister Ella and nephew Paul are always there to read a page and share their thoughts on if brother/uncle John is getting what he wants to get across in the right way. When searching for photographs for chapter two, I was very lucky to have a few people in the community who had my passion for what I was trying to do. Jeff Huber has been in the printing business all his life, and he understood that a few good photographs are priceless gifts.

LuAnn Vander Meulen from the pioneer Fredericks family loves history as much as I do. She spent hours and found some priceless images. After two weeks of going through photographs, Brenda Lange found one jewel that worked. Tom Vermeulen, my competition on eBay for photographs of Ripon, also had the winning information and images that I needed. It was fun working with the two ladies of Palm Avenue, Kathleen Goulet and Ann Betschart, culling through newspapers to find the right answers about their homes. With my undying passion for history, I think I brought other people into the love of it. Steve Enserink let me know that after looking up the history of his house, he and his wife, Shirley, are going to keep looking and unlocking the story of their home. I am so fortunate to live in a community where people care for each other. For people in our town, it is important to help others and share, like the saying that Mrs. Turnquist, the second-grade teacher, had on her board: "It's nice to be important, but it's more important to be nice."

Unless otherwise specified, images in this book are from the author's collection.

Introduction

The character of a city is often recognized and distinguished by the buildings that make up its business district. Sadly, too many cities in our nation have torn down the old, iconic, and beautiful structures only to replace them with indistinguishable cookie-cutter buildings lacking style and personality. Thankfully, the people of Ripon bucked this trend and have preserved much of its past, retaining many of the city's historic structures for us to enjoy. Downtown Ripon today is a vibrant reminder of its past while still changing to meet the demands and needs of a modern city.

All great endeavors need to have an originator, and William H. Hughes was the man who would sow the seeds that would eventually become the city of Ripon. Hughes came to Dent Township in San Joaquin County in December 1857 and purchased 1,300 acres in the fertile valley for his farming and cattle ranch. In 1870, he bought an additional 281 acres that would become the site of the township of Ripon. The late 1860s were a boom time for the railroads, and in 1869, railroad surveyors for the Visalia line of the Central Pacific Railroad were preparing their route for the new line that would connect Stockton to Fresno. By 1872, they had met with Hughes, and he granted them a right-of-way through his property and a parcel of land for a station. The railroad tracks were laid from the delta waterfront of Stockton to the Stanislaus River.

A new train station was erected, along with corrals for horses and cattle, adjacent to the Stanislaus River, and the new city was christened Stanislaus Station. That moniker was not long-lived; it was changed before it had a chance to catch on. In 1874, the new town had a postmaster by the name of Amplias B. Crook, and he felt the town needed a more appropriate title. Crook chose to honor Ripon, Wisconsin. That led to the city of Ripon, California, being officially established on December 21, 1874.

Ripon's development, like that of countless other cities across the United States, directly corresponded with the progression of the railroad. The citizens of the Ripon area had amassed enough capital through successful farming and business to allow for the growth of the new community. This, along with the fact that the city was now linked to a regional transportation network, made Ripon an attractive place for people to put down roots to start new lives in the new community.

Ripon saw its first commercial structures erected in the 1880s. At this time, Main Street in Ripon contained a mix of commercial buildings, blacksmiths, and other small businesses—along with residential housing—scattered up and down the lone street.

In 1884, Ripon had the good fortune of being visited by George Markham. When Markham first visited, there were only 5 business buildings, 14 residents within the town, a small number of pioneer farmers, and a schoolhouse for the community. This was three years before the bridge had been built across the Stanislaus River.

Markham returned to Ripon in 1912, and upon his return, he poured his efforts into the still-young community. He was the founder of a number of buildings that still dot the city to this day. First, Markham built the Markham Hotel, which did double duty as the local grocery store. He then turned his energies toward building the First National Bank, followed by three more brick buildings that would serve the community as various stores. In 1949, he constructed his last building, the brand-new post office.

Buildings seemed to be on the minds of the citizens in 1912. The start of the Markham Hotel initiated a building boom in the city. In four short years, there was a new drugstore at the intersection of Main and Stockton Streets. Down the street from George Markham's buildings, a new grammar school was built. At the same time, there was a residential boom marked by the development of neighborhoods such as the Sunnyside Addition, West Acres, Ripona, and Moulton's Orchard.

By 1917, churches had started to appear on Ripon's Main Street, including the Methodist church, the Congressional church, and the Swedish Bethany Mission Church. Just one block off of Main Street, one could find the First Christian Reformed Church. The small community started to form its own identity with Christian values at the forefront of its image. The ideas of family and faith, intertwined with the daily activity of one's life, started to become a guiding light for the community. For the better part of the remaining century, Ripon's character was formed by such values. Stores were not open on Sunday, and people broke bread with their families on that day. The identity of the community was born, and Ripon became known for its strong values and integrity.

Agriculture was a large part of the origins of the community, and the early farmers of the area became some of its first citizens. These farmers brought with them the hopefulness found in the traditional American go-getter spirit—they would work their way to success. The arrival of the South San Joaquin Irrigation District in 1908 ushered in a new era of farming. Prior to the existence of the irrigation district, much of the area farming was dry farming, which mainly involved grain and cattle grazing. The arrival of water meant that crops that needed regular irrigation could be now farmed. J.P. Watkin's 1902 experiment of growing almonds in the region was wholly embraced, and Ripon was on its way to becoming the almond capital of the nation.

With the advent of irrigation, Dutch migration to Ripon really hit its stride in 1917. Newspapers in Michigan and Holland told of the opportunity of prosperity with the arrival of water. A church was in place for religious needs, and the land was ripe and beckoning for them to work. The cultural diversity and the agricultural mix of Ripon continue to change, with growing communities of Portuguese, Swiss, and Italian people. These immigrants shaped the look and feel of Ripon throughout the 20th century. Their faith, value in community, and strong work ethic all became evident in the growing community, and they still help uphold the city to this day.

CHAPTER 1

Let's Go Downtown

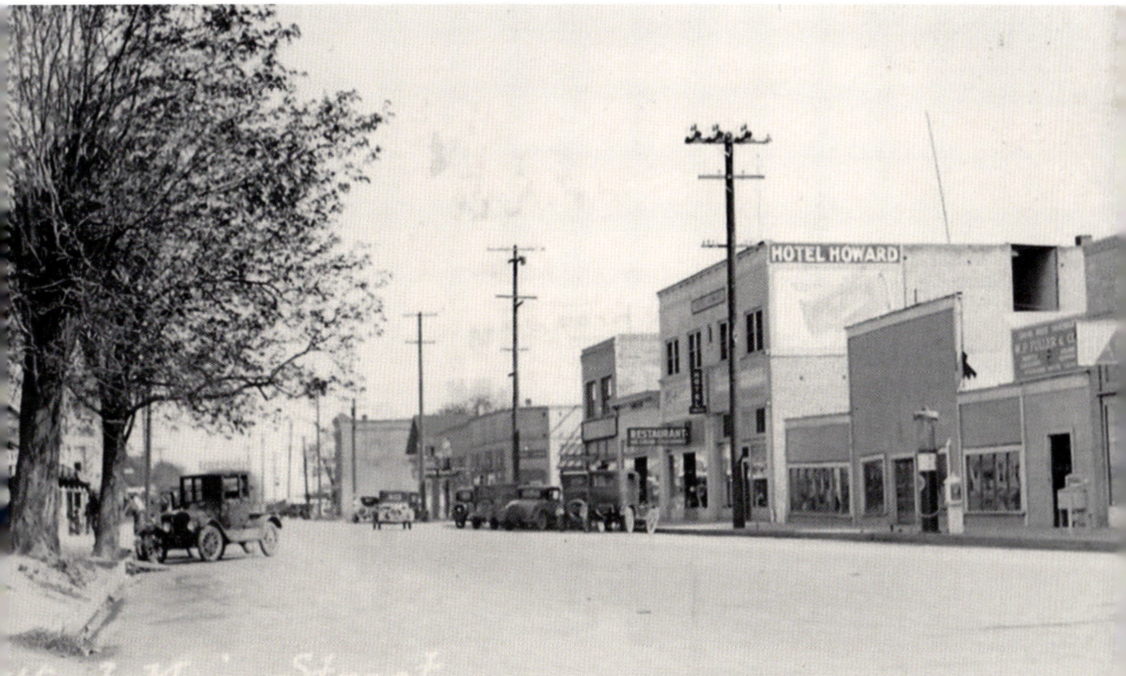

Ripon was a leader in retail in the early years. In the 1920s and 1930s, Ripon had five grocery stores, eight gas stations, a car dealership, two barbershops, a cleaners, a men's and women's clothing store, a hardware and appliance store, two hotels, three bars, and four restaurants. When people wanted entertainment, they would take the train to Ripon. This chapter will look at how the retail heart has beaten over the years in the brick and mortar of the community.

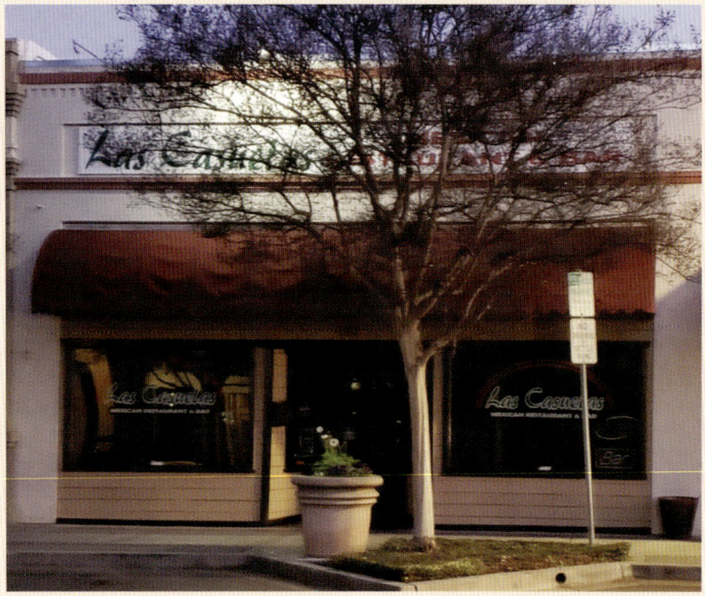

This building was constructed on speculation in 1921 by entrepreneur Hans Madsen. The building was 30 by 110 feet, and the first business to occupy this space was the Ripon Hardware Company. It was followed by a duckpin bowling alley in the early 1940s, and on July 6, 1944, after World War II, the Rio Theatre moved into the location. After the theater closed, the building was used for an assortment of business offices, and then its life as a restaurant began. Pie and Berger was the first restaurant, followed by others, and finally, it became Las Casuelas Mexican Restaurant.

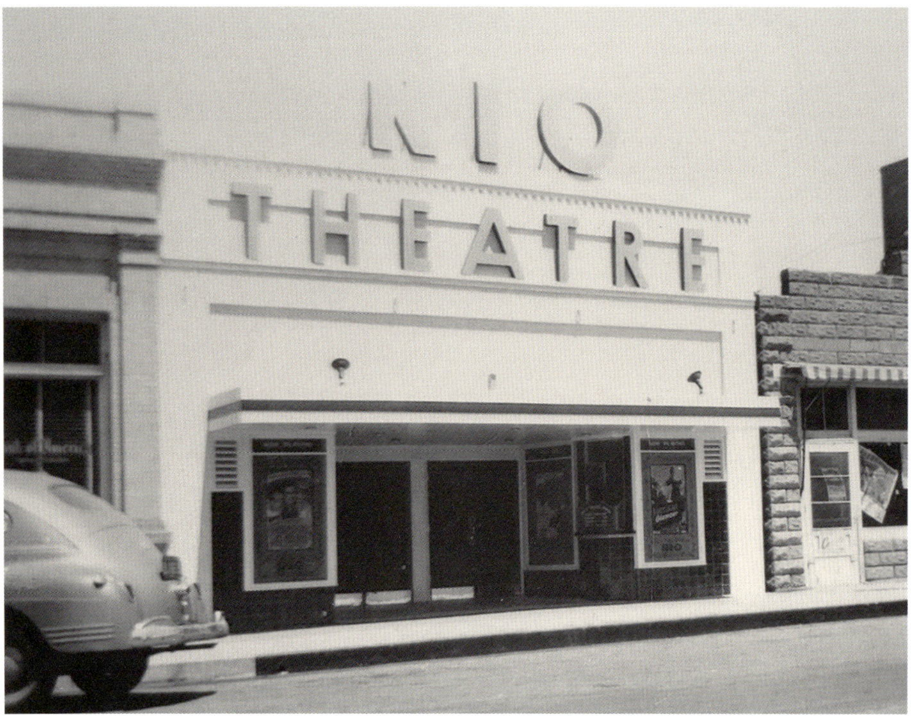

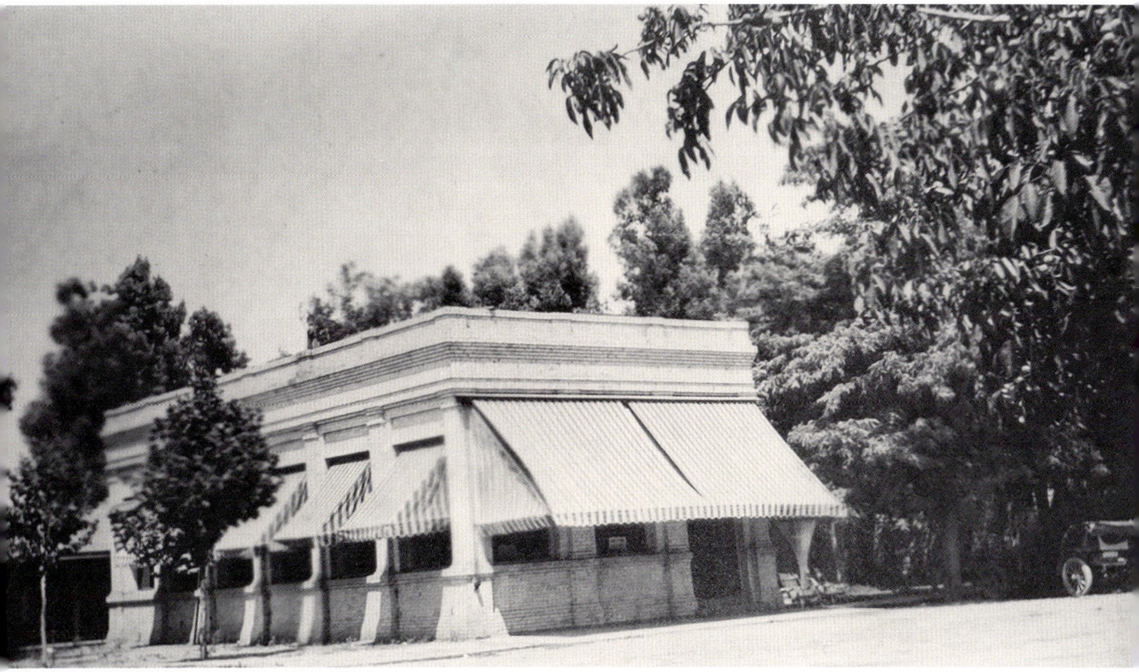

The Bank of Ripon was organized on March 16, 1910, by a group of leading residents and two North Dakota bankers. The bankers were visiting San Joaquin County, and their business partners were showing them around Ripon. The bankers decided Ripon would be a good location for a new business venture. The cornerstone of the Bank of Ripon building, which was designed by Stockton architect Walter King, was laid on April 9, 1910.

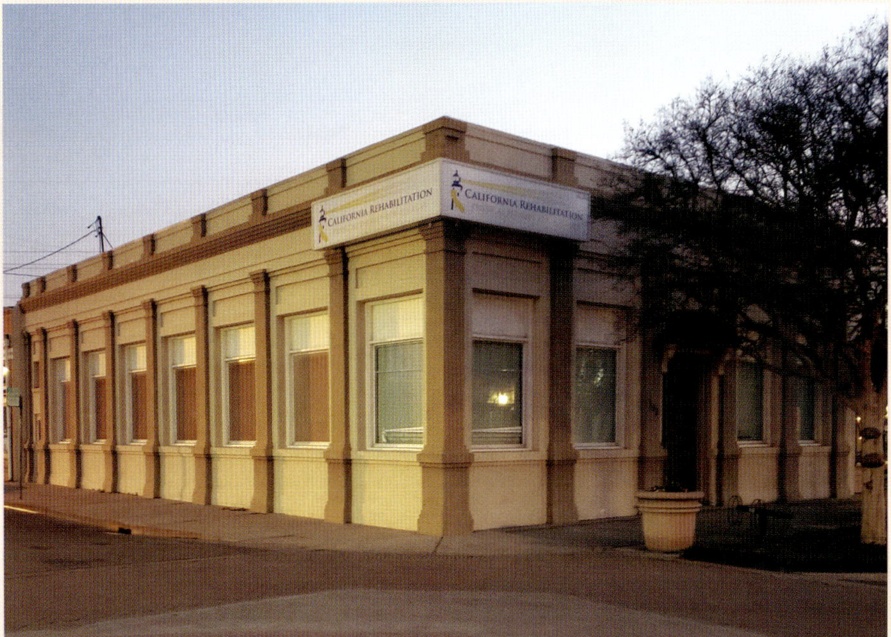

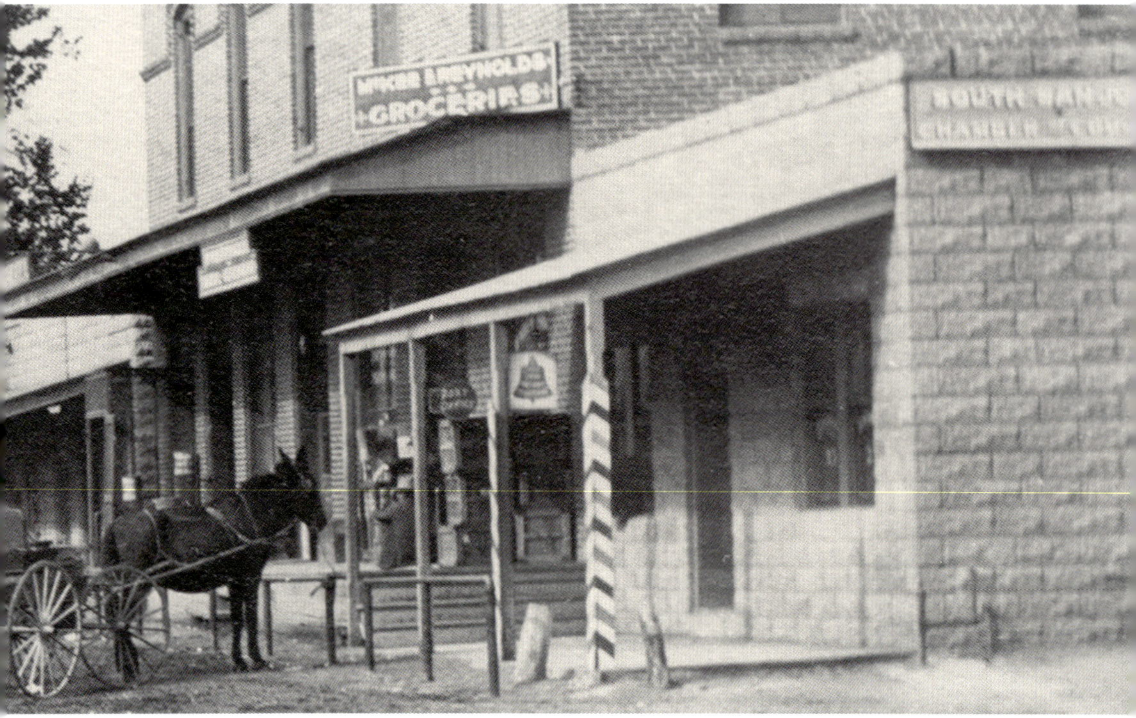

The single-story masonry structure located next to the Odd Fellows building was erected around 1895. In earlier photographs, one can see the hitching posts that sat in front of the building. It served as Ripon's post office in 1908, as well as the telephone exchange, a beauty shop, a real estate office, the Bright Spot (a saloon), and the offices of the South San Joaquin Chamber of Commerce for a bit of time. Around 1933, the small masonry block addition was constructed on the eastern side of the building.

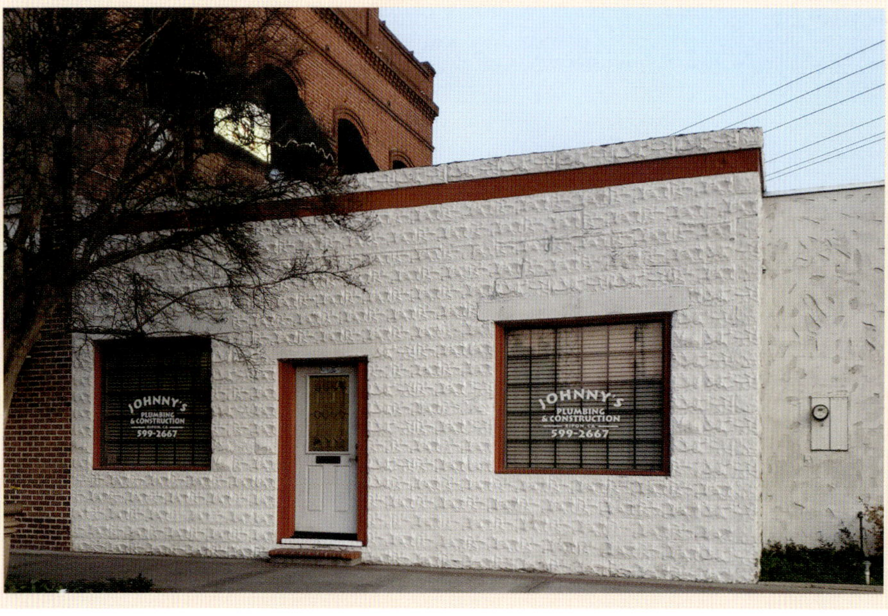

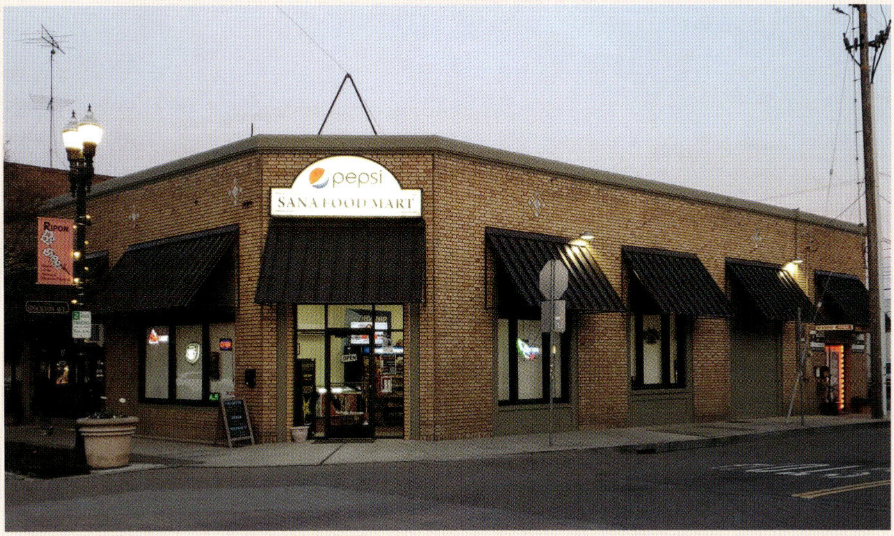

Ripon pioneer builder George Markham's home sat at this location and was moved to First Street in 1920 to make way for the construction of the First National Bank. In August 1921, the contract was awarded to local building S. Trondhjem, and work was immediately started on the 30-by-60-foot structure. The corner entrance originally had large oak doors that were able to swing both ways. The bank opened in December 1921. The building later housed a grocery store, millinery, interior design studio, and another grocery store.

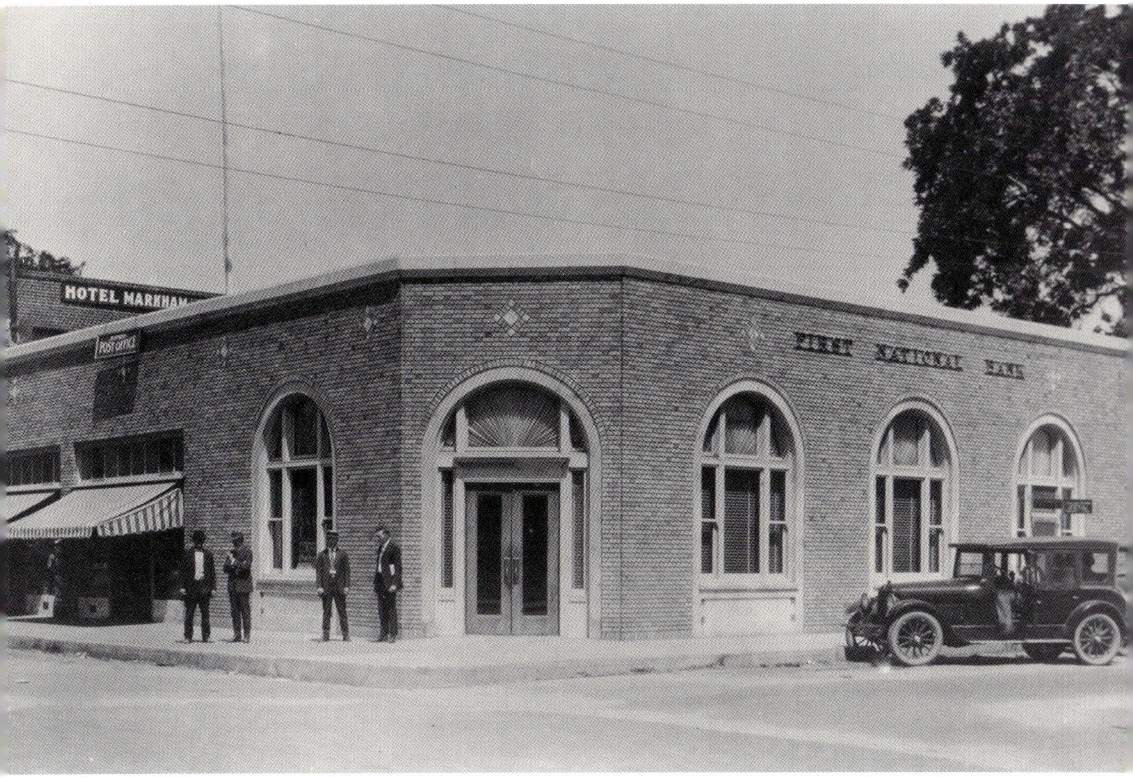

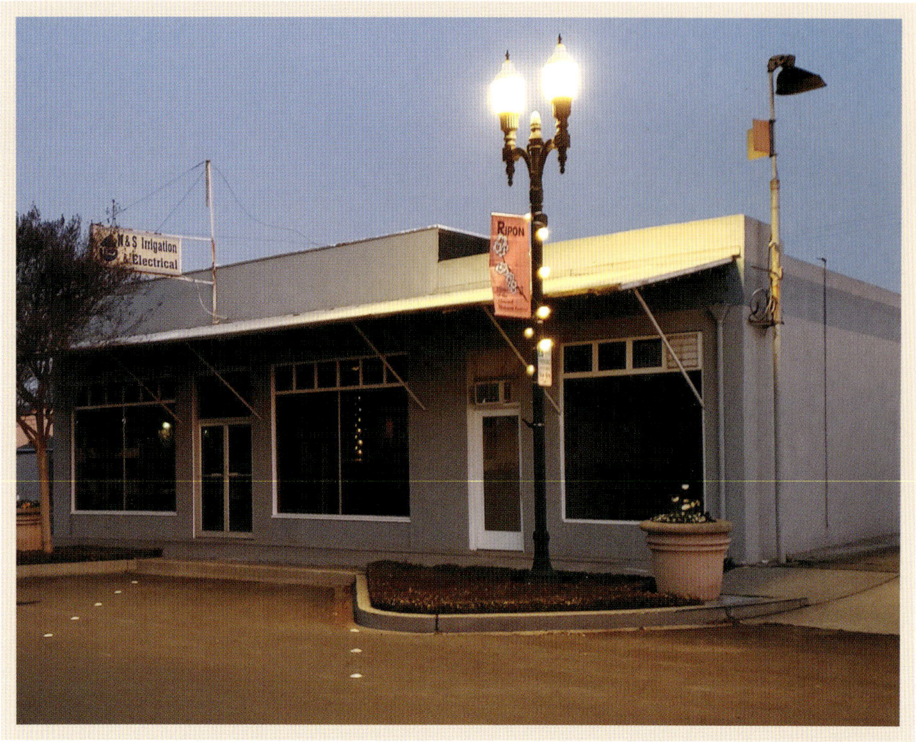

This building was erected in 1912. The west side of the building was used as a bakery, and the east side was used as a grocery store. Starting in the 1920s, it was used as a commercial laundry. In 1930, it was the Van der Beek Shoe Hospital. In 1936, the Van Dyken brothers moved into the building with their new business, N&S Home Appliances; the name of the business comes from the first letters of their names (Nick and Sam). This was one of the first commercial buildings to occupy this block.

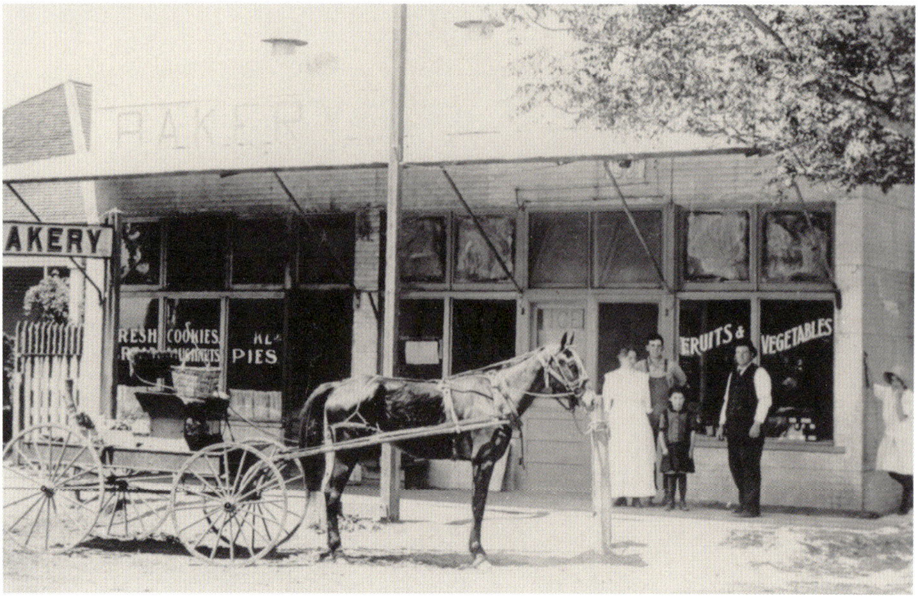

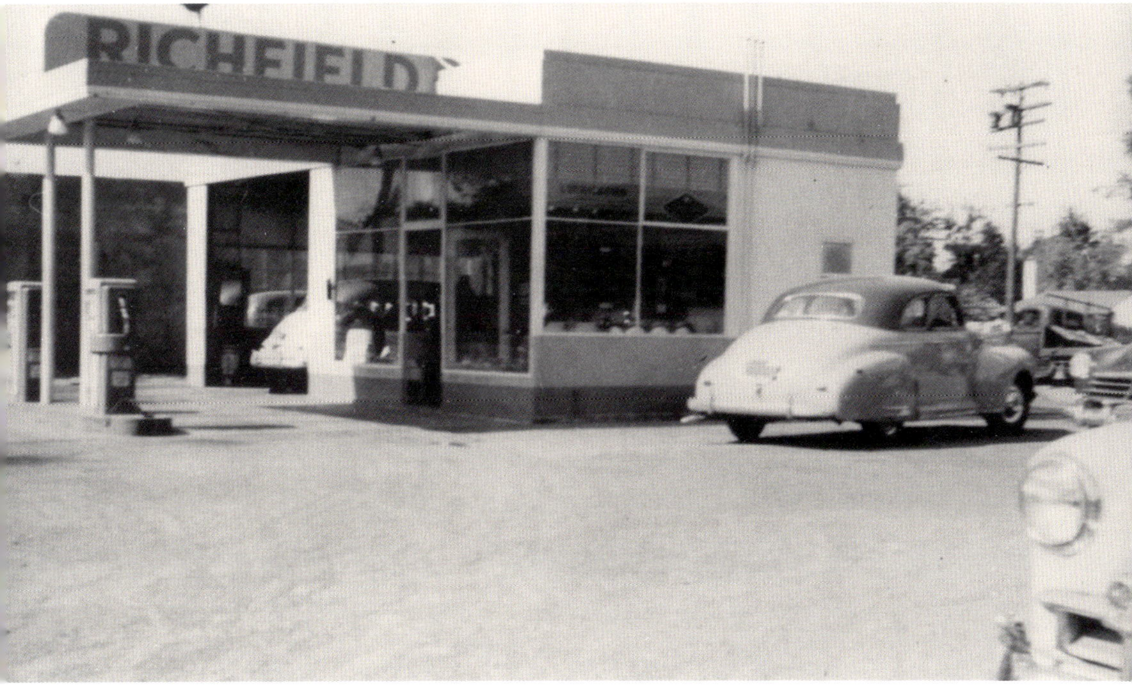

This address has probably crushed the entrepreneurial spirit of more individuals than any other address in Ripon. On July 14, 1949, the new Richfield service station opened under the management of Robert Muir. Before a year had passed, in September 1950, Joe Smink took over ownership of the service station. Eight gas stations dotted the streets of Ripon at this time, and profitability must have been a challenge. The station continued to change hands nine times from 1951 to 1972, with Red Helms being the last owner.

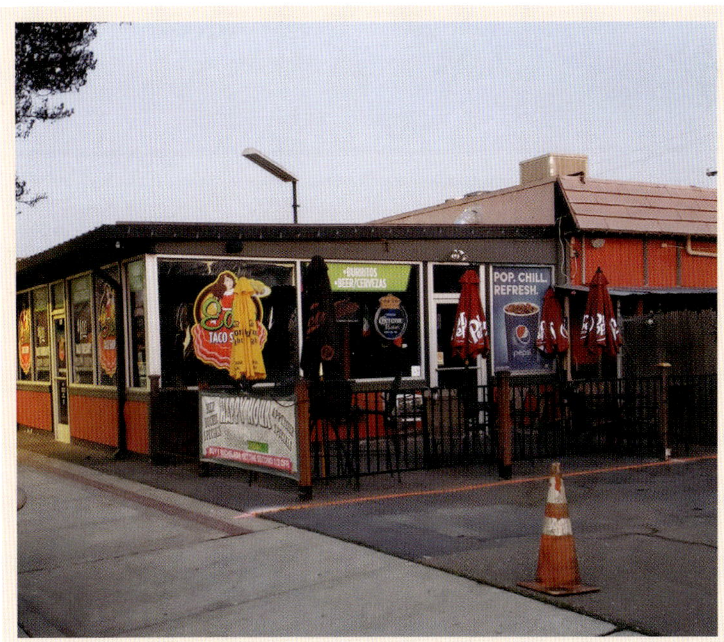

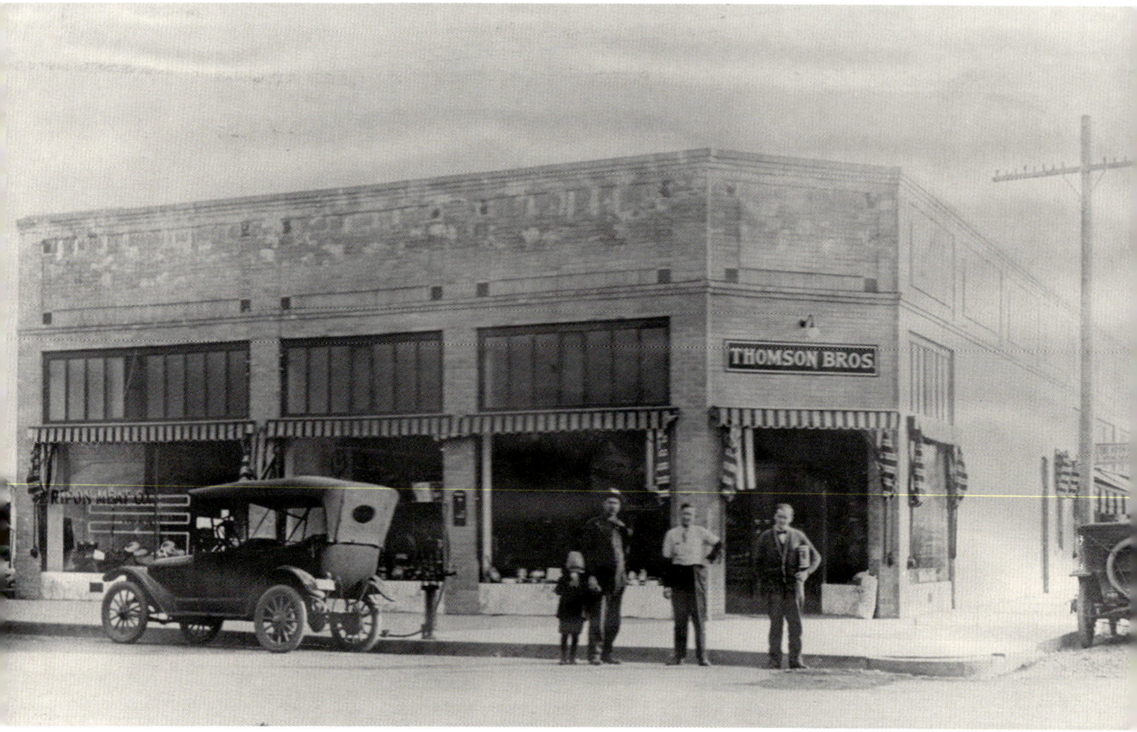

Construction of the Madsen & Peterson building was started in February 1916. Hans Madsen was a building contractor, and Peterson was the financial end of this project. The building was divided into many storefronts. The Ripon Meat Market would occupy the three retail spaces facing Main Street, while Dr. Ned Gould's office occupied one space on Stockton, and the other area was a barbershop. The next tenants were the Thomson Bros.; they occupied the space until 1922. Heine Spaman and Greg Osborne bought them out and opened Osborne and Spaman grocery. (Past image courtesy of the John Wever family.)

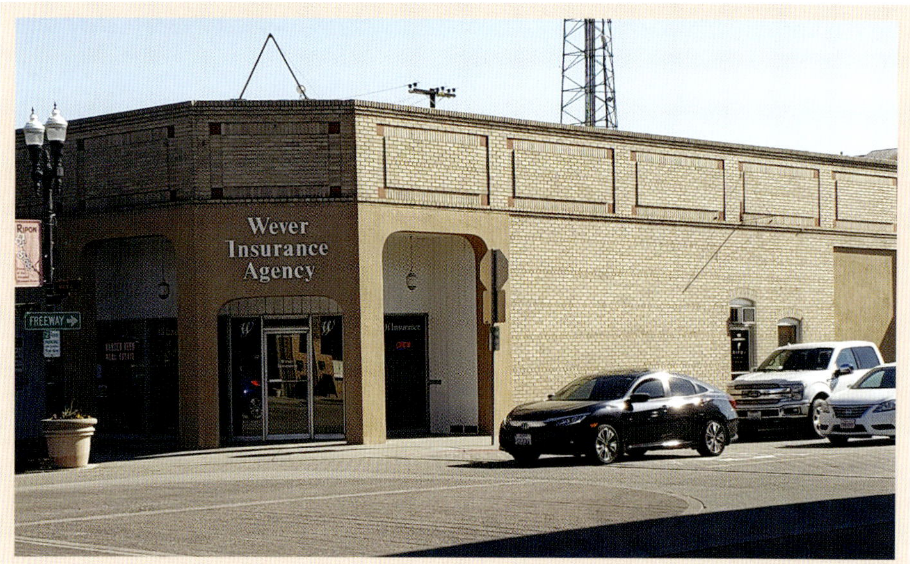

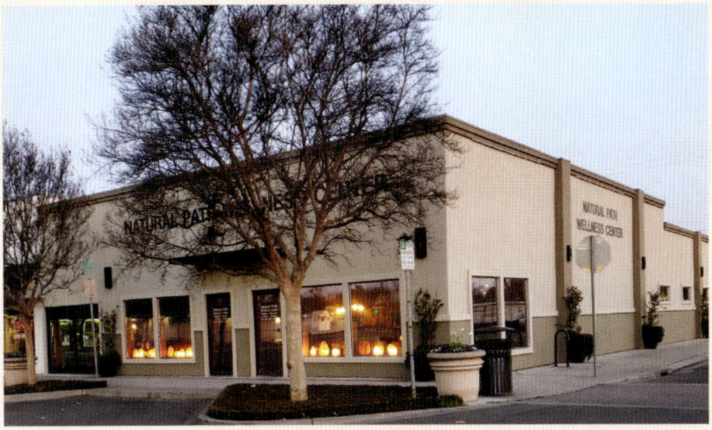

In 1951, Ripon Dry Goods & Furniture opened in this new building and had a nice run. In February 1962, Mary and Jesse Franklin opened Franklin's Department Store. From 1984 to 1991, food took center stage with the opening of Pizza Plus. In 1992, health was the answer, with Ripon Chiropractic Clinic. The current tenant of this building is the Natural Path Wellness Center.

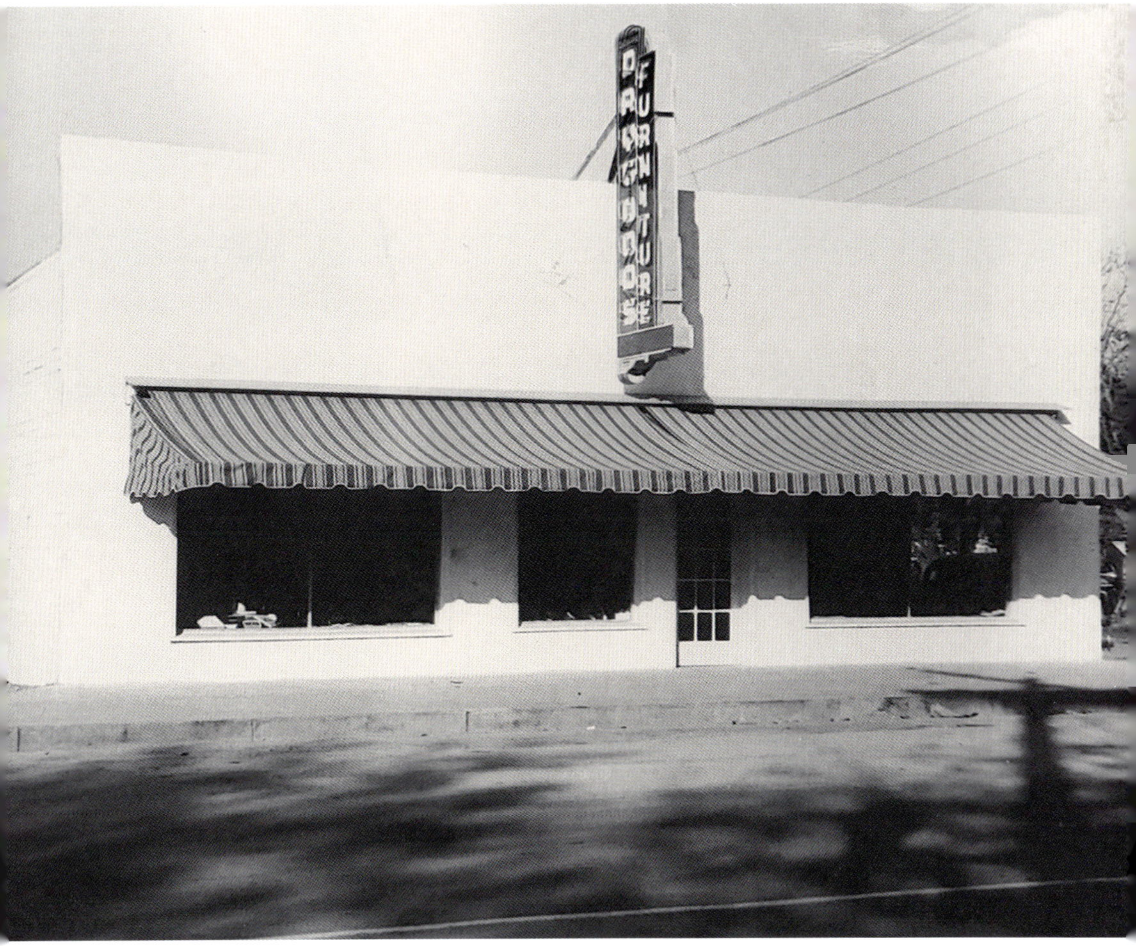

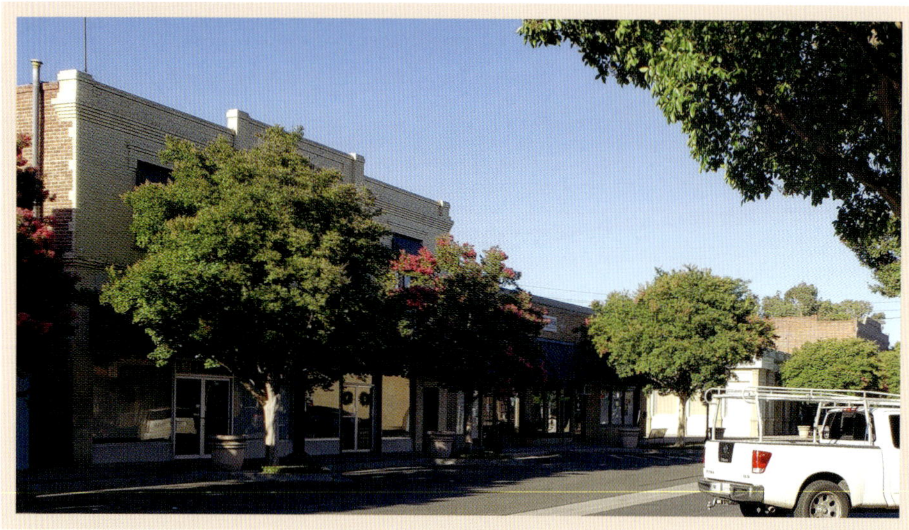

Many historical buildings remain in Ripon. The one at far left in these photograph is Markham Hotel. The building on the corner was the First National Bank, and it is now a grocery store. The round-topped building and the Hughes real estate building were moved around the corner to Stockton Street, making room for Markham's new post office and haberdashery buildings. In the following block are the Bank of Ripon and the large, stately Odd Fellows building (at the very end of the street).

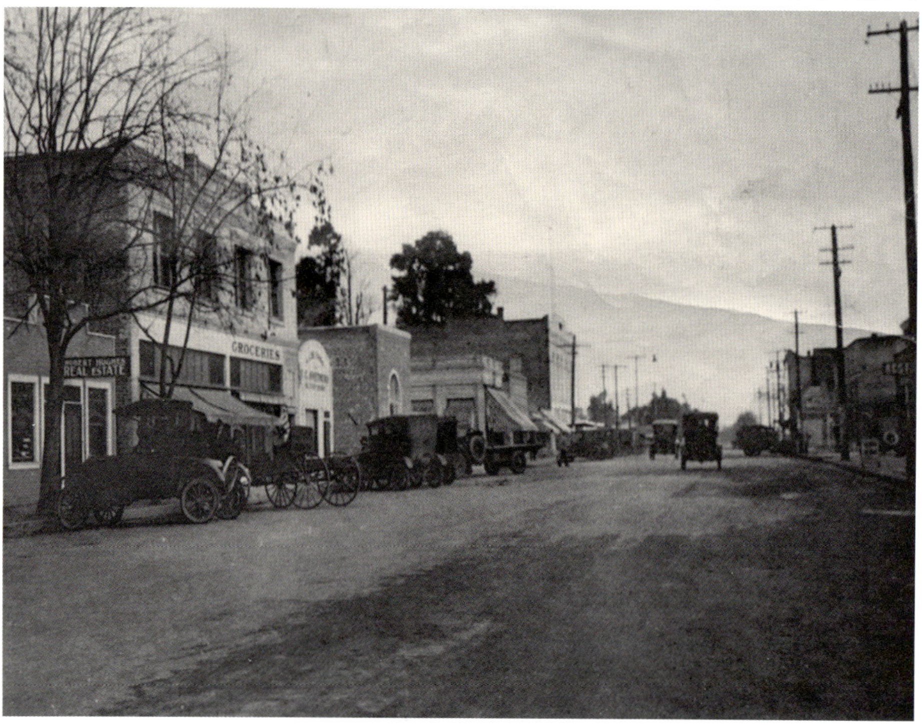

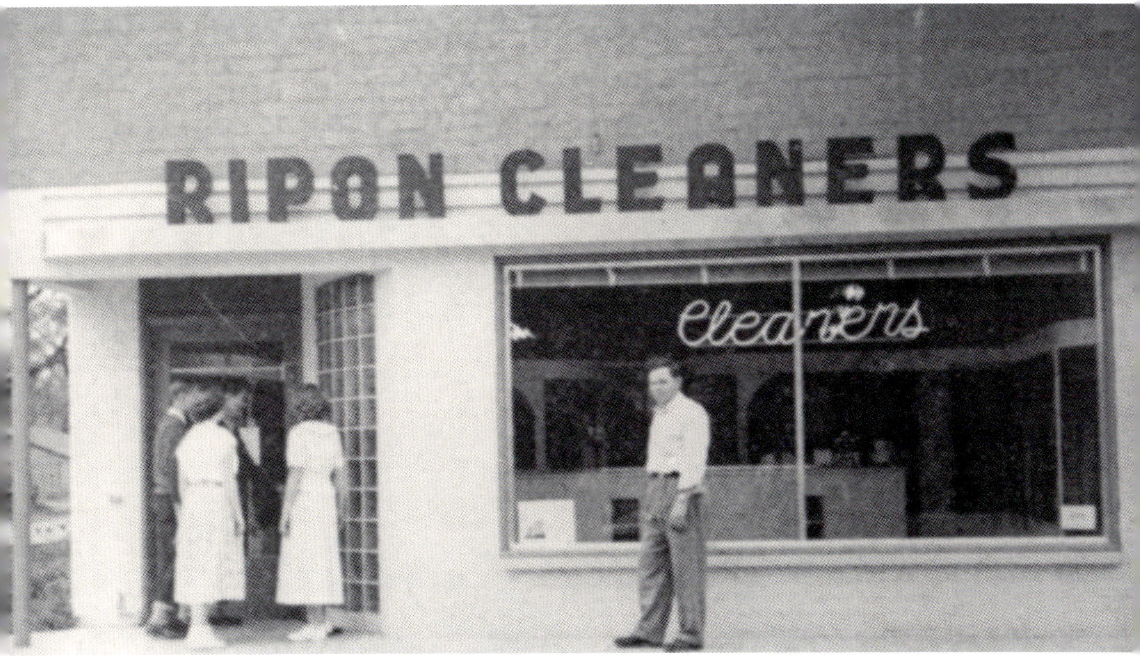

Ripon Cleaners was opened by Teekell Shelby in 1947. One year later, it was purchased by Ralph and Mary Atwell, becoming a part of the Ripon landscape. In June 1958, Vogie Loon stepped in for the retiring Atwells, running Ripon Cleaners until 1963. The new owner was the nephew of the Atwells, Alden Atwell. Sadly, in 1966, Alden passed away; his widow then ran the business. In 1972, Bernie Engen took over, operating it successfully until 1995. In 1998, Tracy Schaffer opened a martial arts school in this building.

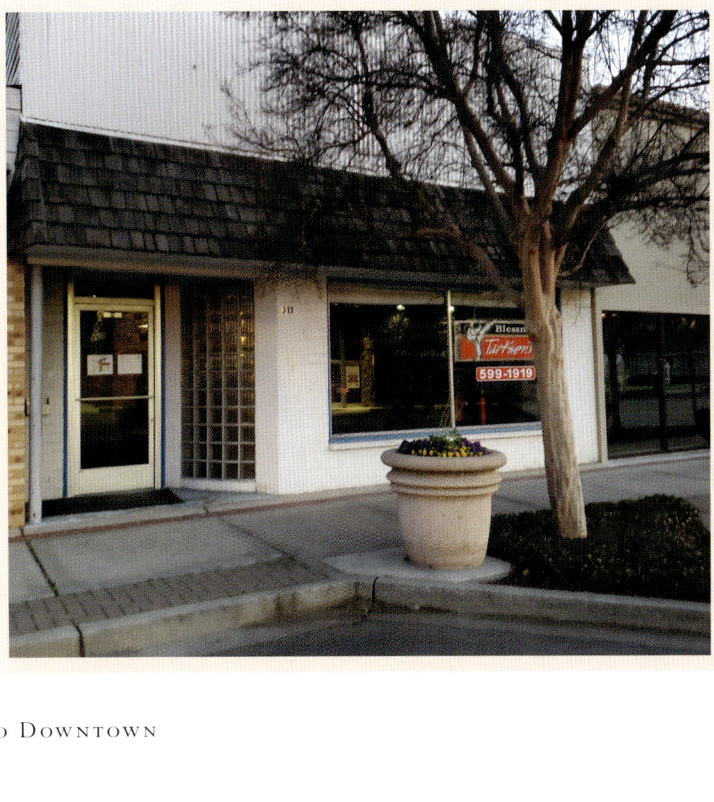

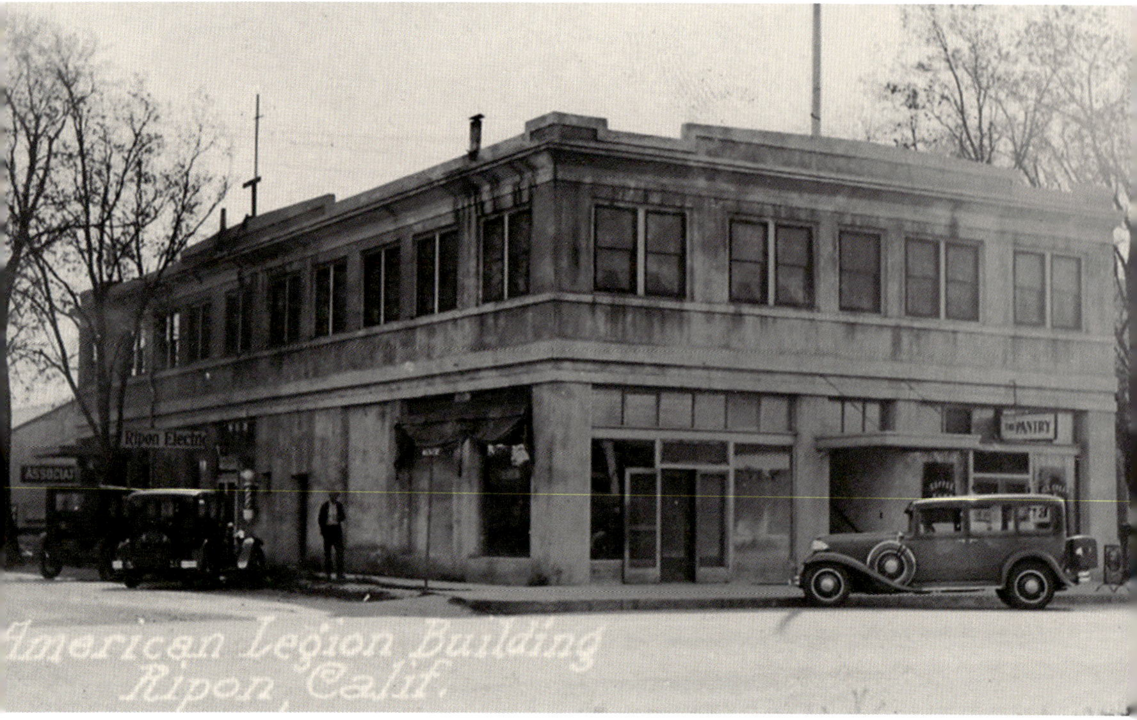

The American Legion building was dedicated on November 27, 1928. The general contractor was George Thompson, and the architect was George N. Hilburn. It was built for $25,000, with only 52 members in the post. It had four apartments on the second floor and a banquet hall for 200 in the basement. It soon became apparent that keeping a building of that size was not financially feasible. The American Legion moved to a new hall on Stockton Street in April 1938. In 1952, this building was moved across the street to allow the fire department to expand.

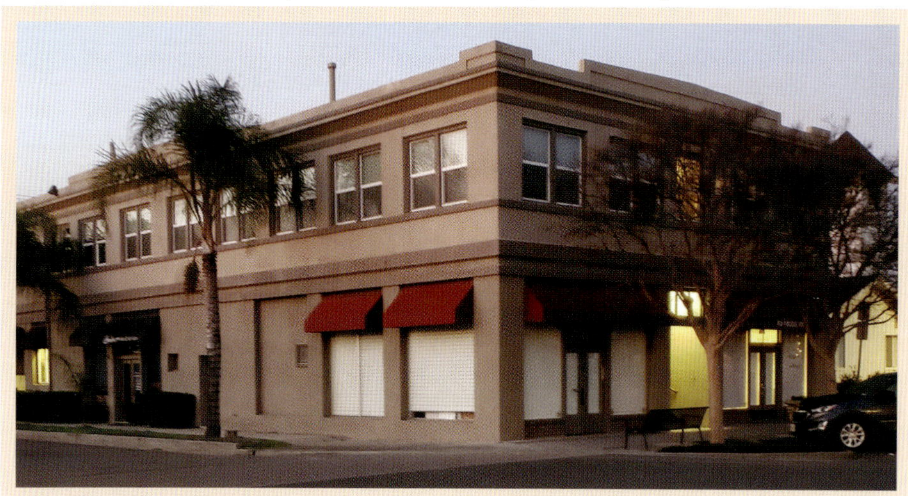

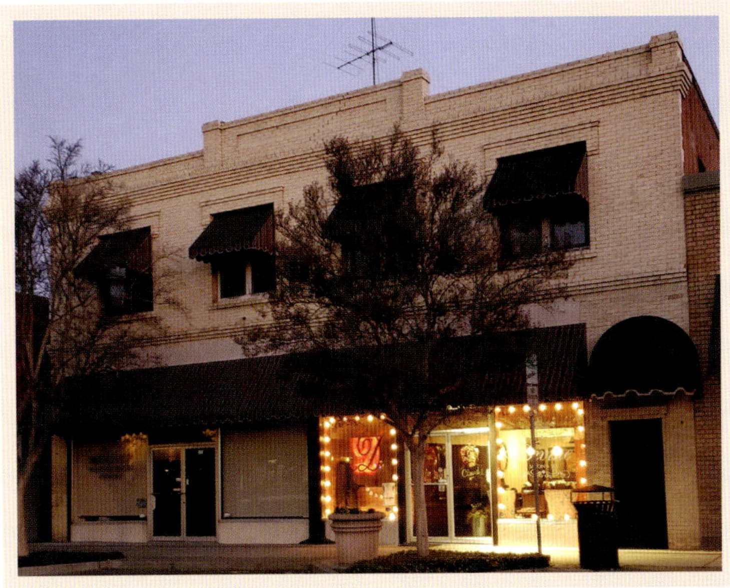

In 1912, there was a movement to get a first-class hotel in Ripon. Everybody suggested that Molly Markham would be the perfect person to run this hotel with her brother George. In April 1912, excavation began on the basement and foundation of the 50-by-80-foot Markham Hotel. The first floor had 2 retail spaces, and the upper level had 16 hotel rooms. The hotel cost $10,000 to build. Molly ran a café on one side of the first floor, and August Lindblom and J. Emanuel Johnson ran a clothing store on the other.

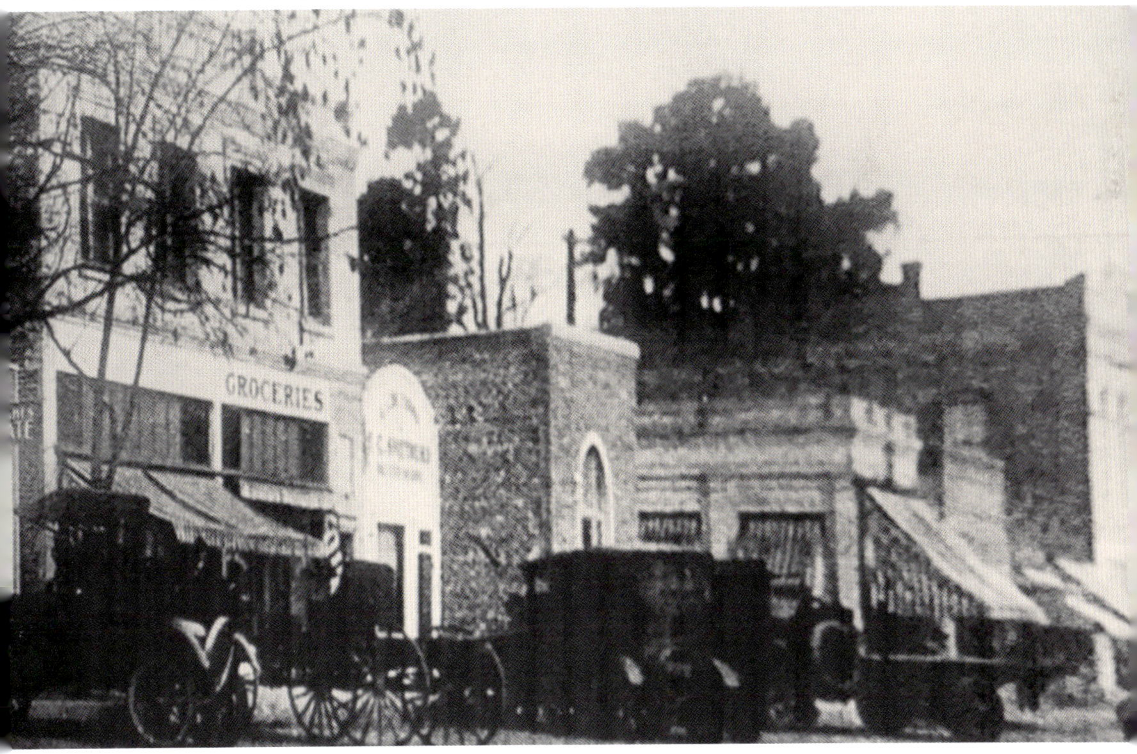

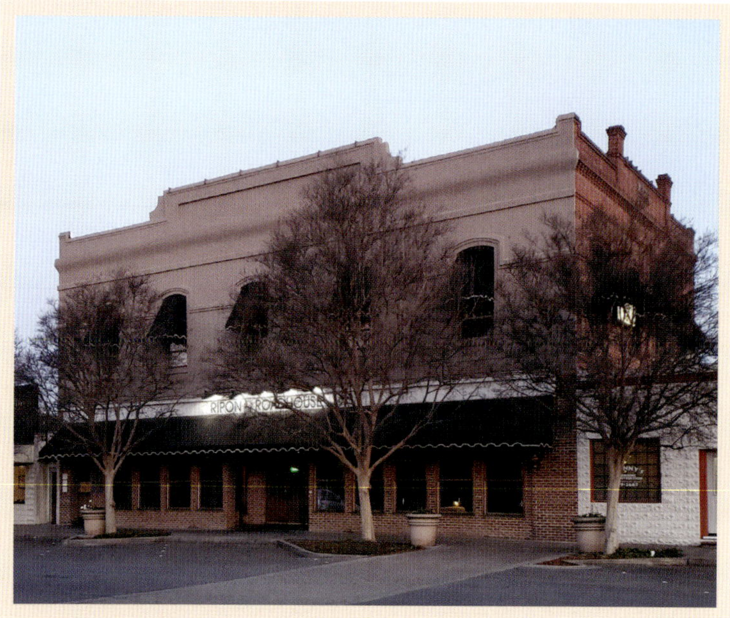

The Odd Fellows building was erected in 1886 and housed the McKee and Reynolds Mercantile on the ground floor. The IOOF Lodge was on the second floor. This was the second substantial brick building constructed in Ripon, with the first being the Riddle building in 1884. This building has had many tenants through the years. Starting in 1986, restaurants have occupied it. Thanks to the efforts of Bob and Ann Ide in 1983, the building was preserved for future generations.

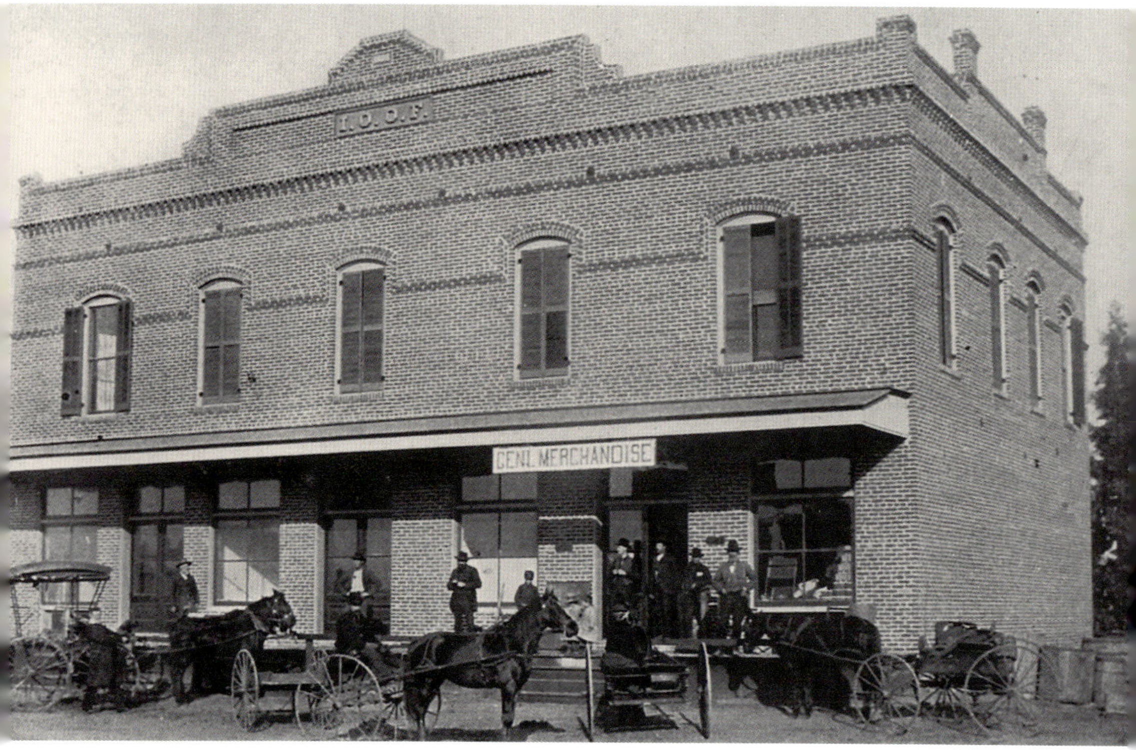

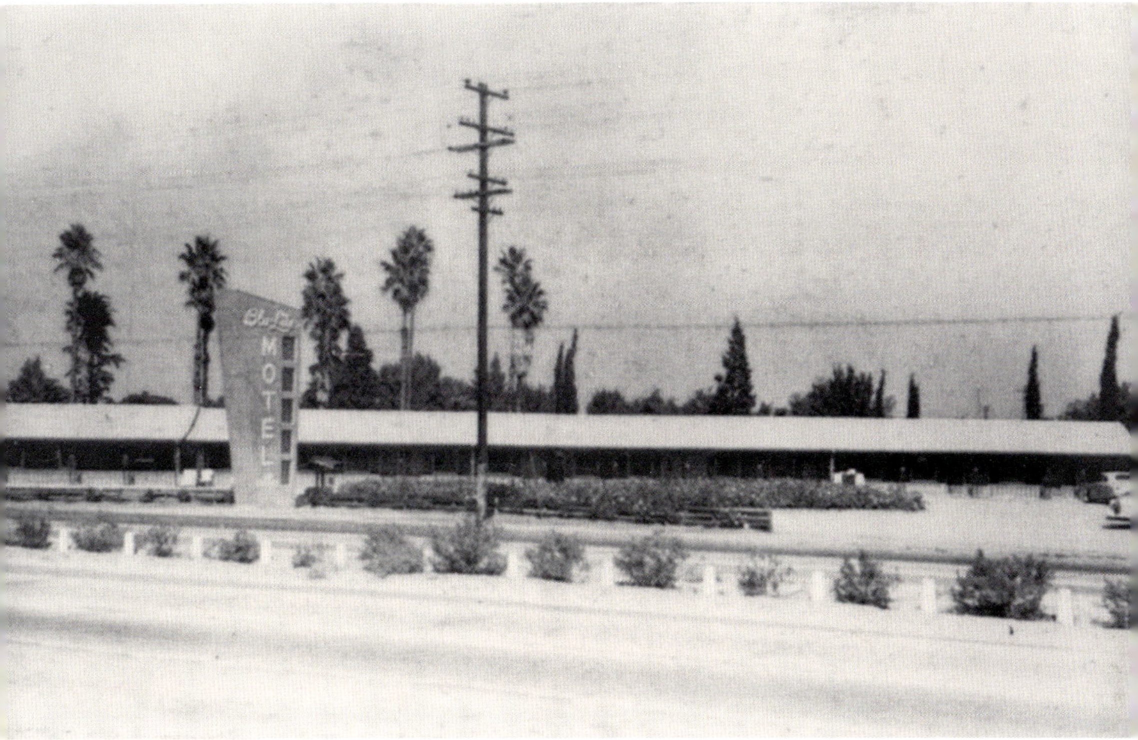

A motel sitting next to the Ripon Cemetery may seem peculiar to some, but if they know the history, it makes sense. The cemetery association owned the property upon which the Blue Light was built. The property was sold to Floyd Stevens. The Blue Light motel opened on June 28, 1952, at a cost of $50,000. Just one year later, in 1953, Dot and Harvey Latscha took ownership of the motel. The hotel was refurbished by the Latschas in July 1956. In 1964, the iconic sign and landscaping were lost to progress.

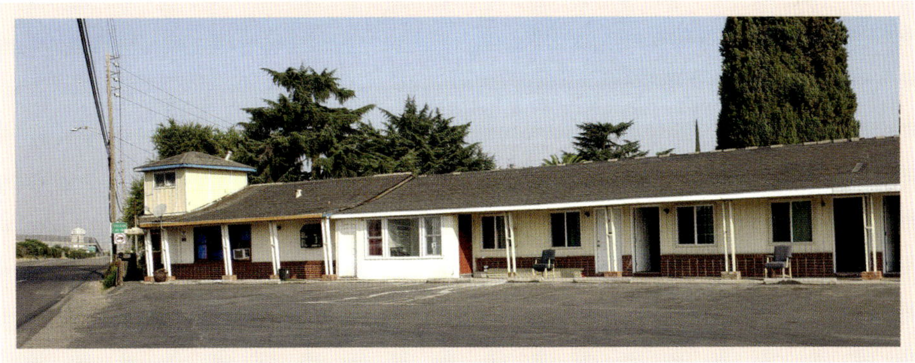

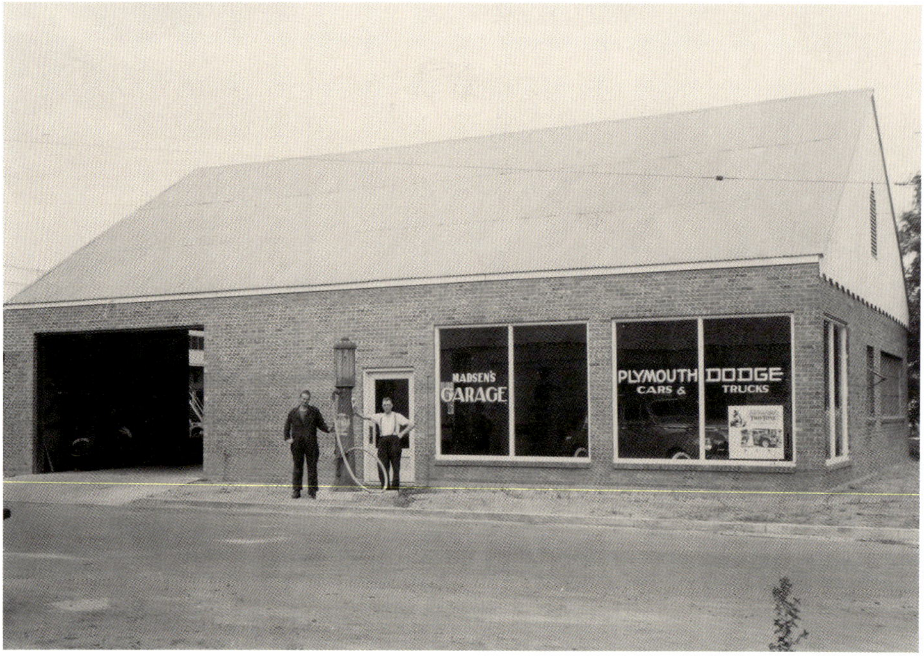

In 1951, Madsen's Garage served as a dealership for Plymouth and Dodge cars. But even back then, Hans Madsen realized that selling was not as profitable as fixing cars. With this idea, Madsen opened a service garage to repair the cars that he sold. Madsen was one of the first businessmen to start to build on Walnut Street. Soon, he owned the whole block, with buildings from First Street to the end of Main Street. This location is now Magpie Antiques.

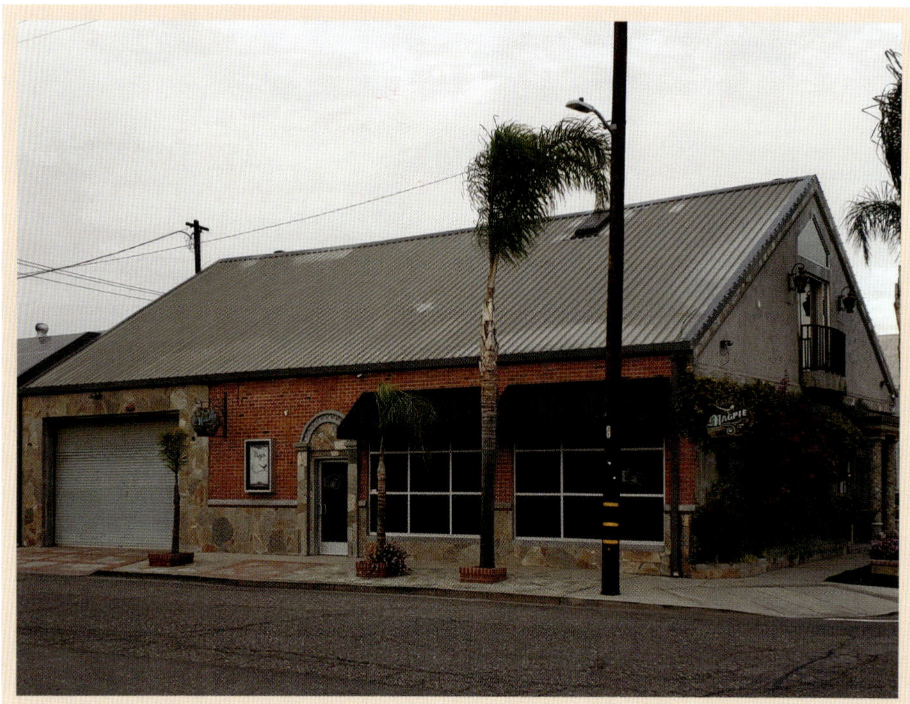

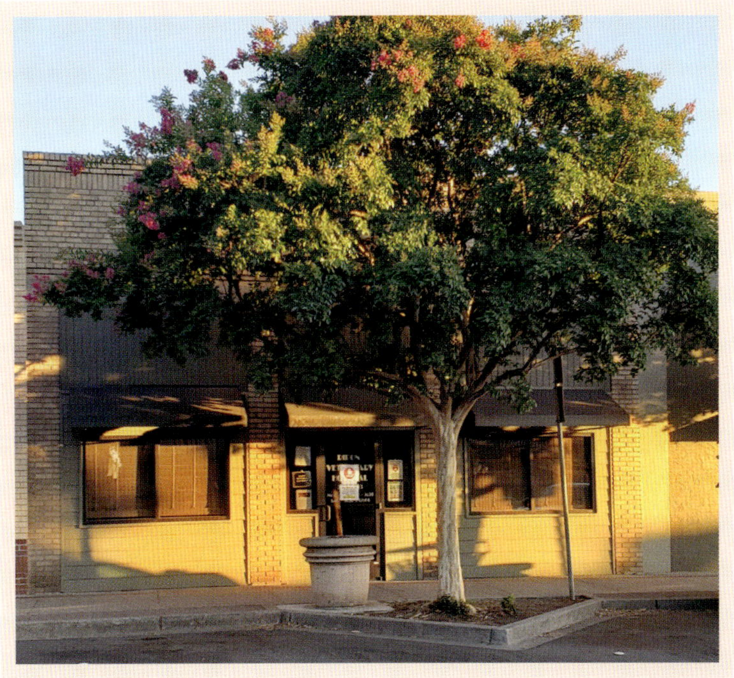

The Davis Bros. Hardware Store, owned by George and Harold Davis, was both a necessity and a novelty. Harold, who worked behind the counter, was nicknamed "Lum," while his brother George was often called "Abner." The Davis brothers bought the A.J. Nourse Hardware Store in 1919 and grew the business. In 1923, Hans Madsen built three more brick buildings for the Davis brothers, tripling the size of the business. George was an astute businessman, graduating from Heald's Business College. Two of the brick buildings that Madsen constructed are now home to a veterinary hospital. (Past image courtesy of the Huber family.)

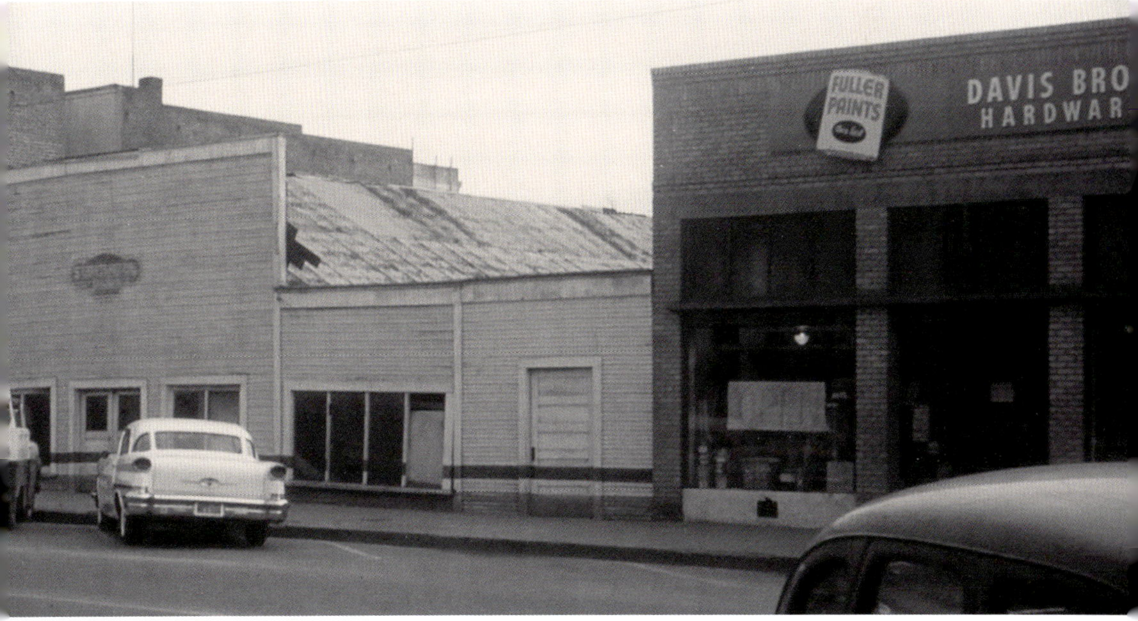

This jail was constructed in 1925 and used by Ripon constable John Garrison and the county sheriff; architect Ralph P. Morrell designed the building. Ripon contractor L. Ubels built the jail for $2,498. It was initially erected on a lot on North Walnut Street at the intersection of the railroad right-of-way. On December 3, 1957, it was raised off of its foundation and moved to its current location at First and Locust Streets. The aerial photograph below shows the jail in its original location.

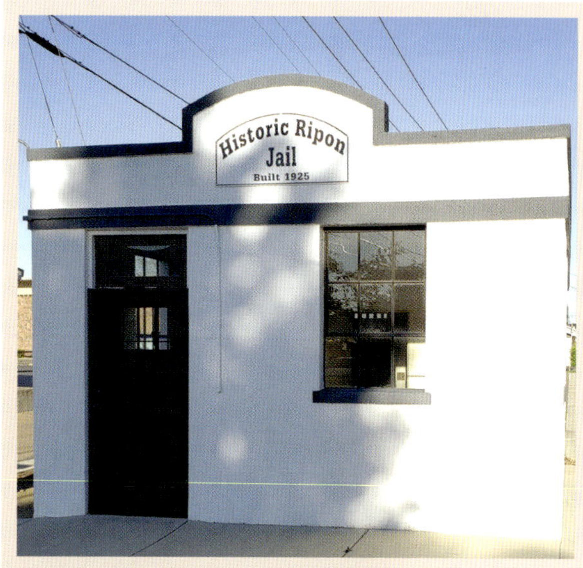

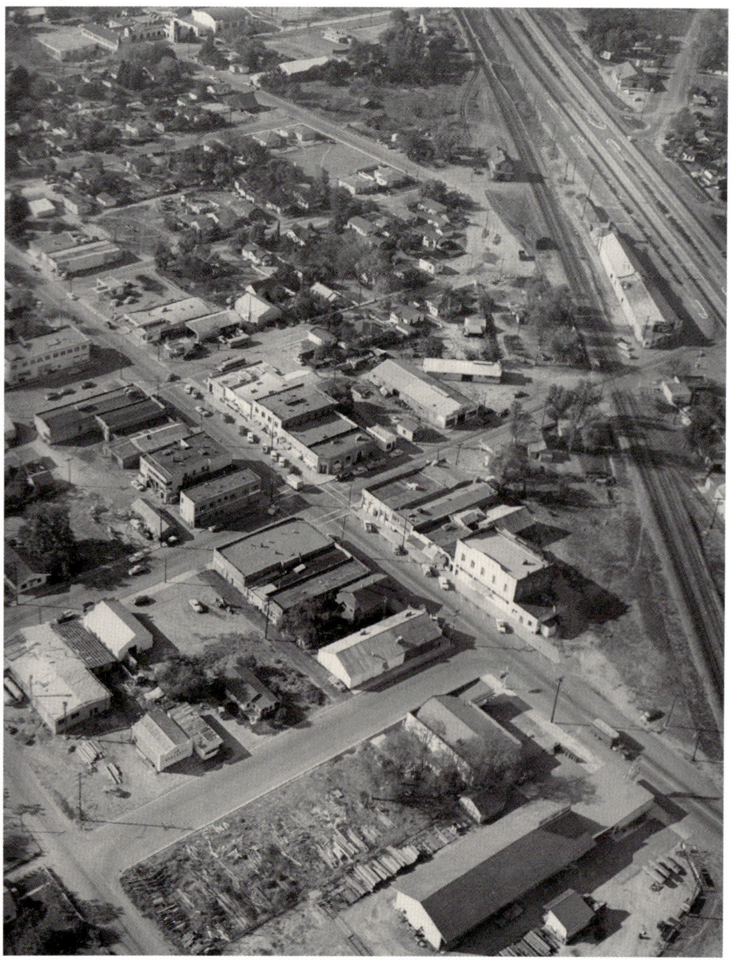

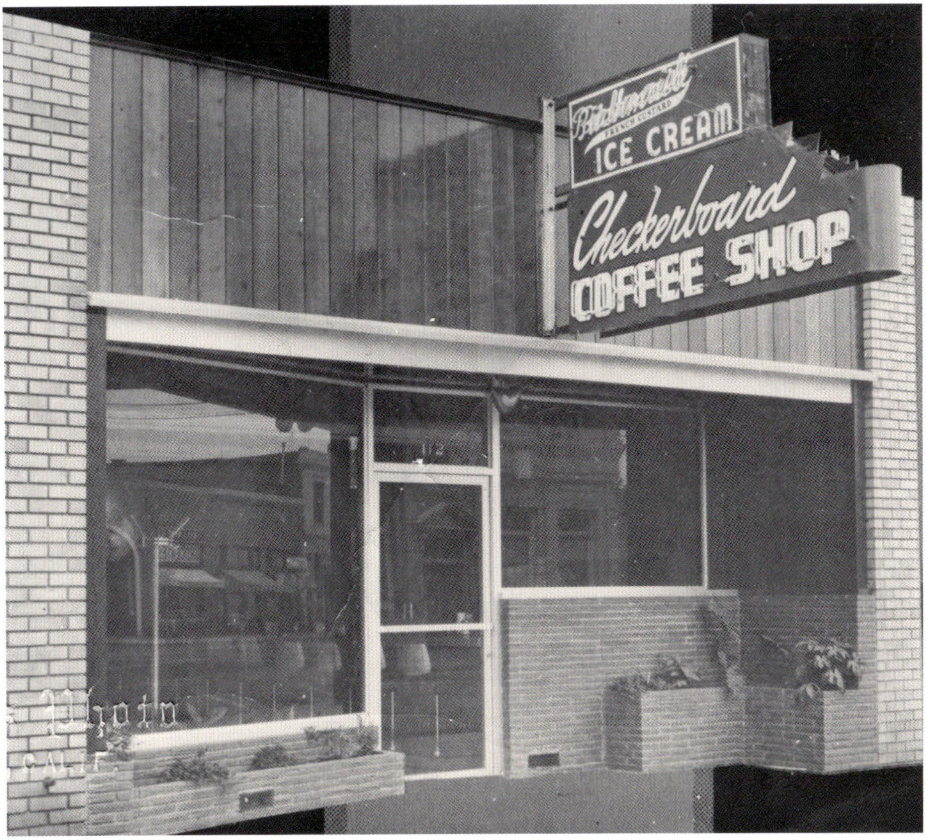

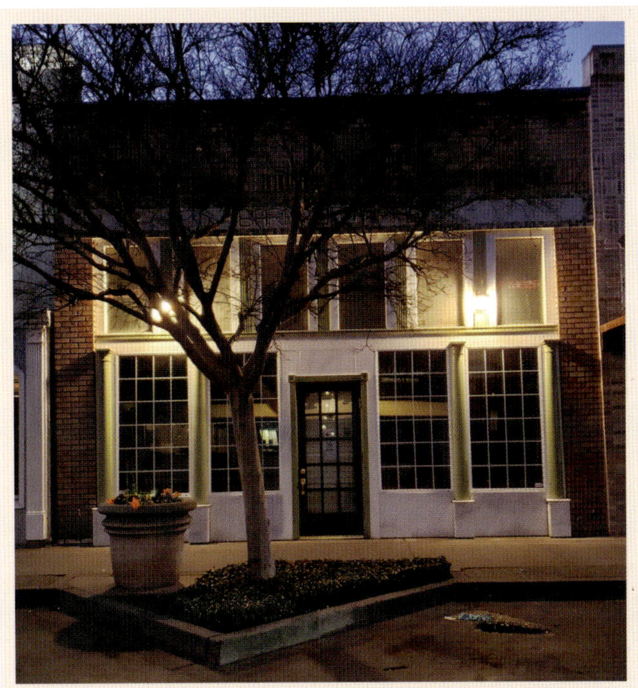

In 1934, Klass Vermeulen opened his shoe repair shop. In 1947, Spurr Jewelry opened; later, the store changed hands, becoming Worley Jewelry in 1948, then moved across the street, becoming DeBoer. In 1957, Doc and Ida Allen spruced up the place and opened the Checkerboard Coffee Shop, keeping the good citizens of Ripon fed for many years. In 1963, Bob Lange opened a restaurant in the building and ran it successfully for many years. In 1979, Art's Floor Covering took over. When Art VanGinkel decided to retire in 2011, it was sold to Barnwood Arms.

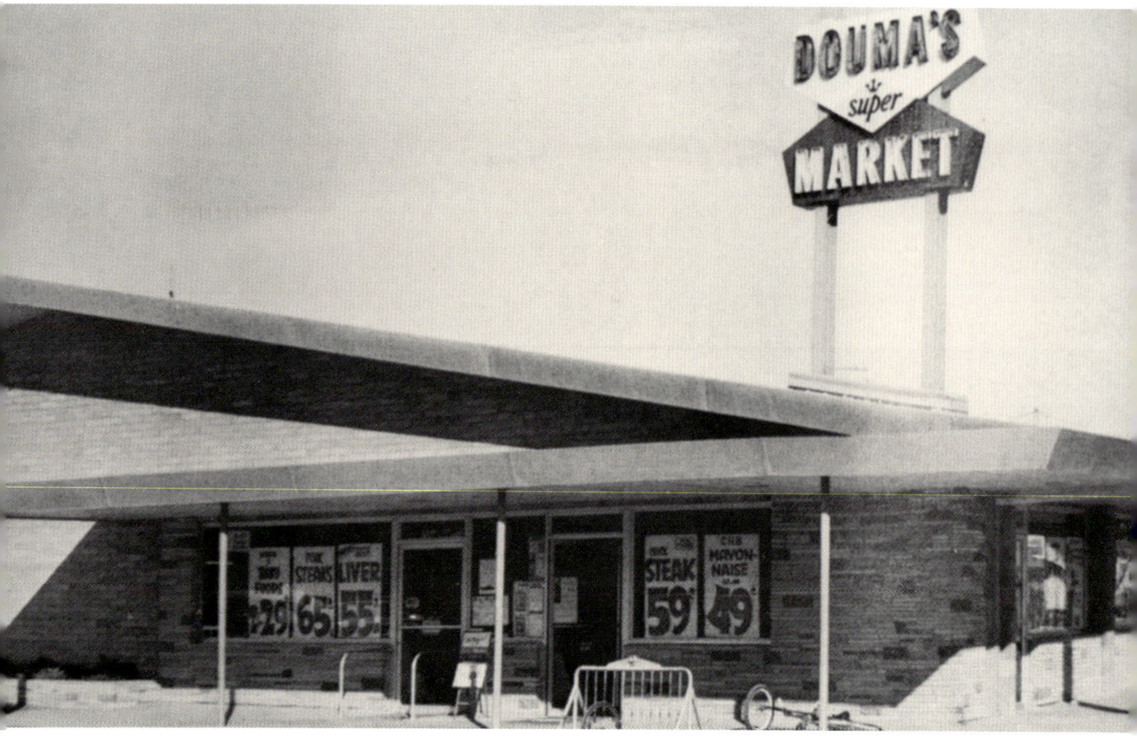

The Douma family left their imprint on Ripon starting in 1919. The family's first market occupied a space in the Markham building. In 1951, it was moved to a Quonset-style building. In September 1962, the doors opened on a 7,000-foot supermarket with all the bells and whistles. When the Doumas retired in 1968, Mar Val grocery took over. In 1990, Mar Val moved to a new shopping center. The Schemper family, another industrious Ripon family, remodeled the old structure into a hardware store. When the Schempers moved the business to their own center, it became the library.

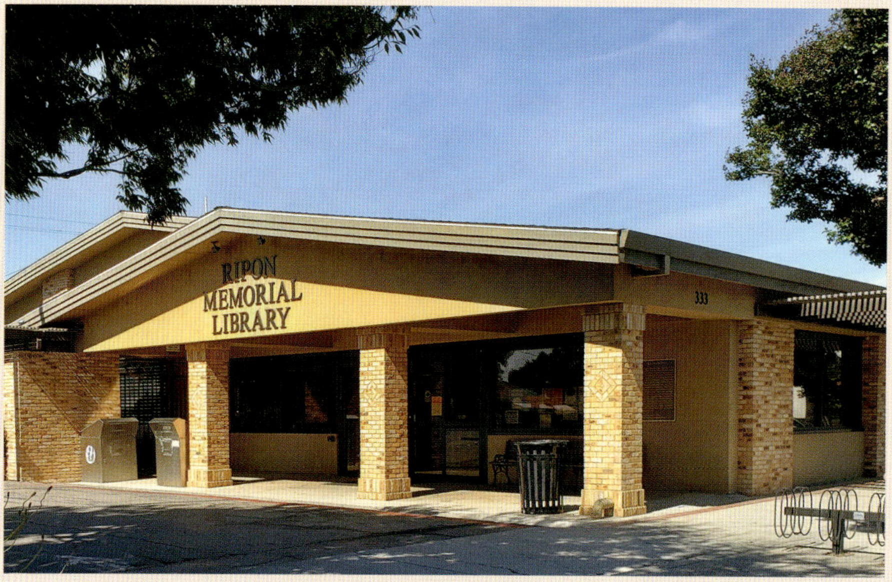

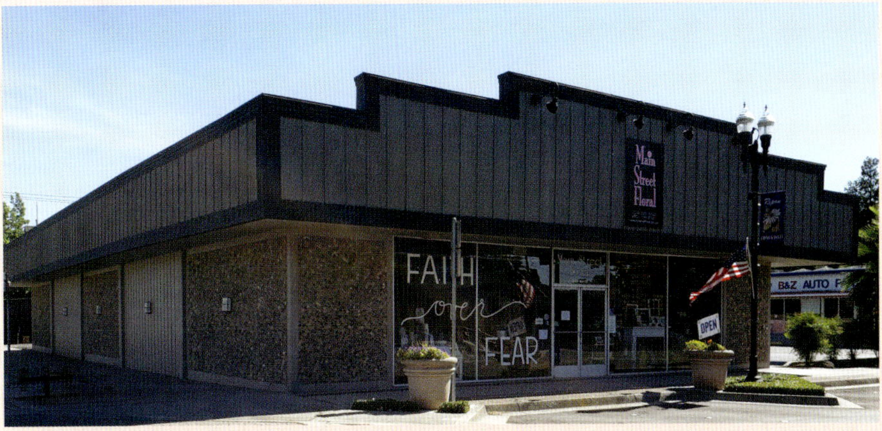

In 1962, Dale Larson began his career as a pharmacist in Ripon by becoming a partner of Ripon Drug on the corner of Main and Stockton Streets. Ripon Drug had been a part of the Ripon business district for more than 45 years. In May 1965, Larson built a stunning new pharmacy that was state of the art for its time. When Dale and his wife, Phyllis, chose to retire, the building was bought and turned into Main Street Floral.

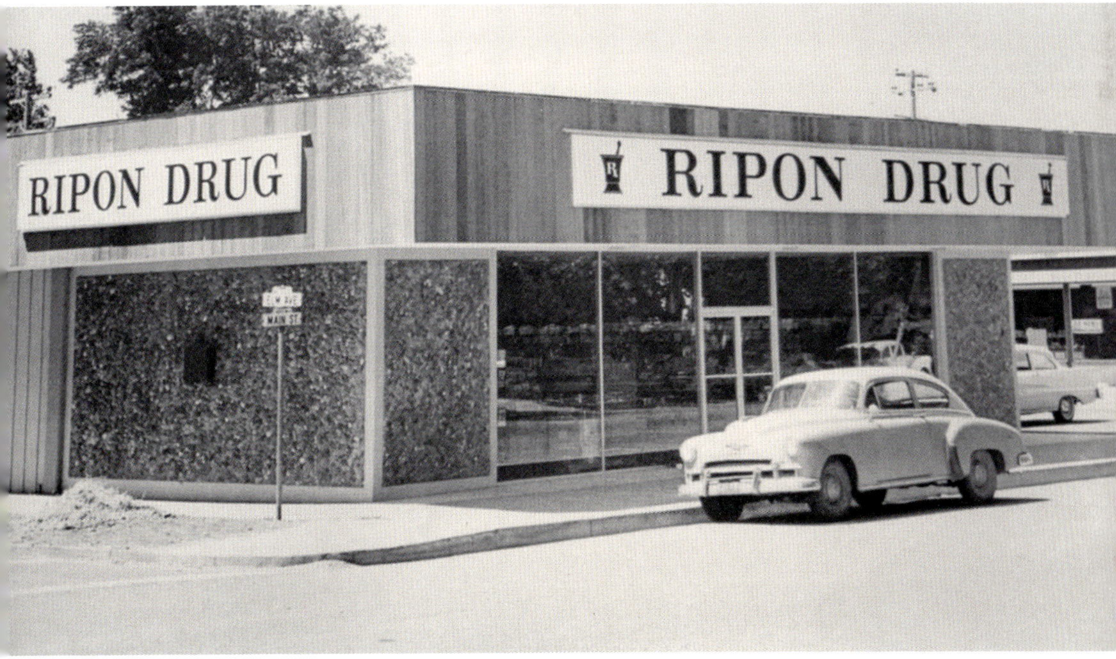

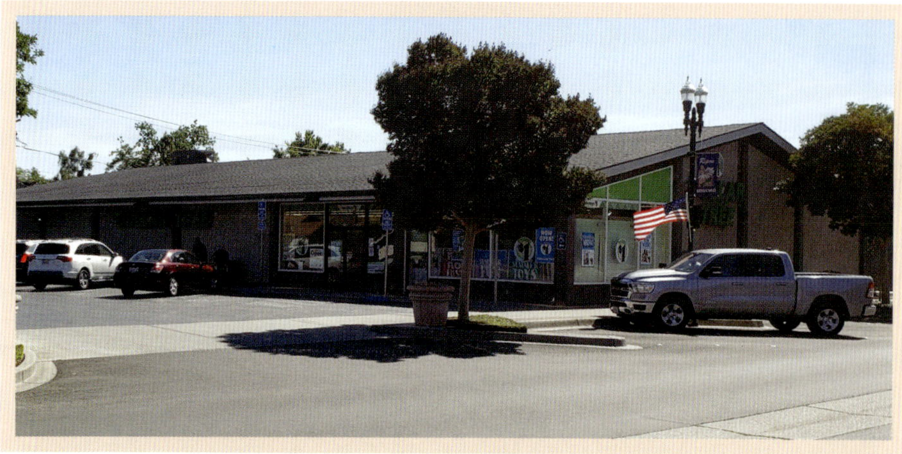

In February 1962, George Bledsoe opened Big G Food Center; that year, Ripon residents had six grocery stores to choose from. In May 1964, Bob Van Slyke, along with three other locals, became the new owners, changing the name to City Food Center. In March 1976, Gee Gong rebranded the store as National Market. In 1988, Gong died, and Bruce Healds opened Healds Market. In 1996, Joe Phillips and Joe Vega opened Cardio Club Fitness, which operated here for the next 22 years. In 2018, Dollar Tree brought retail back to the location.

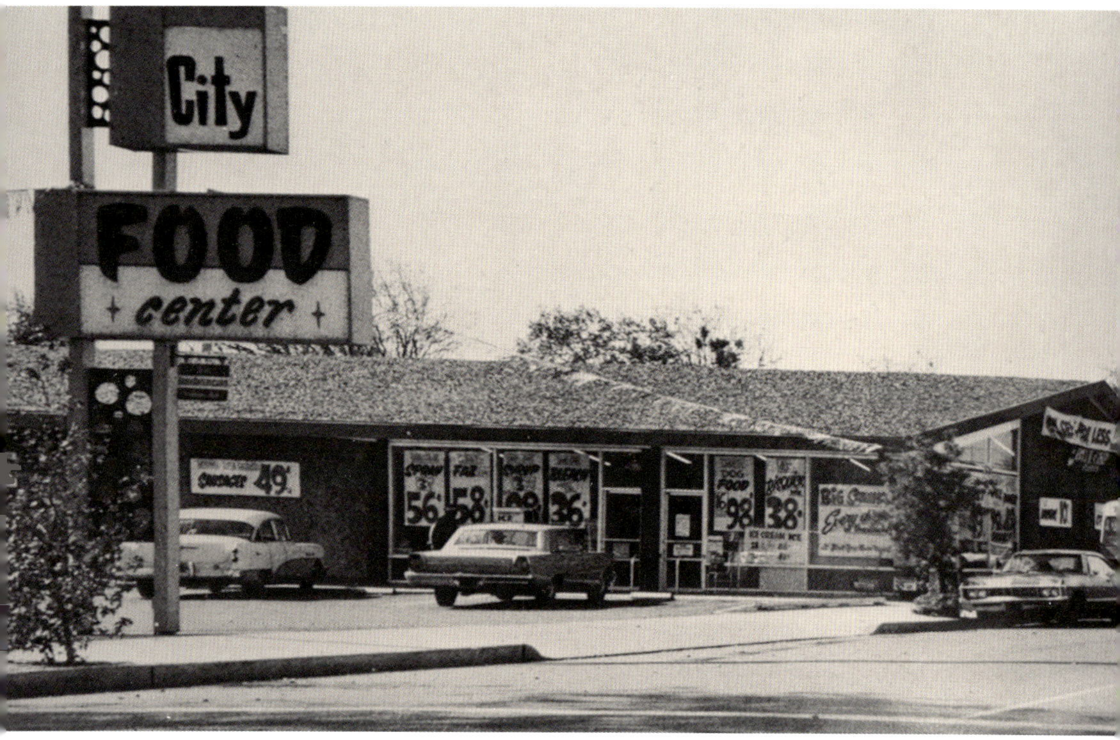

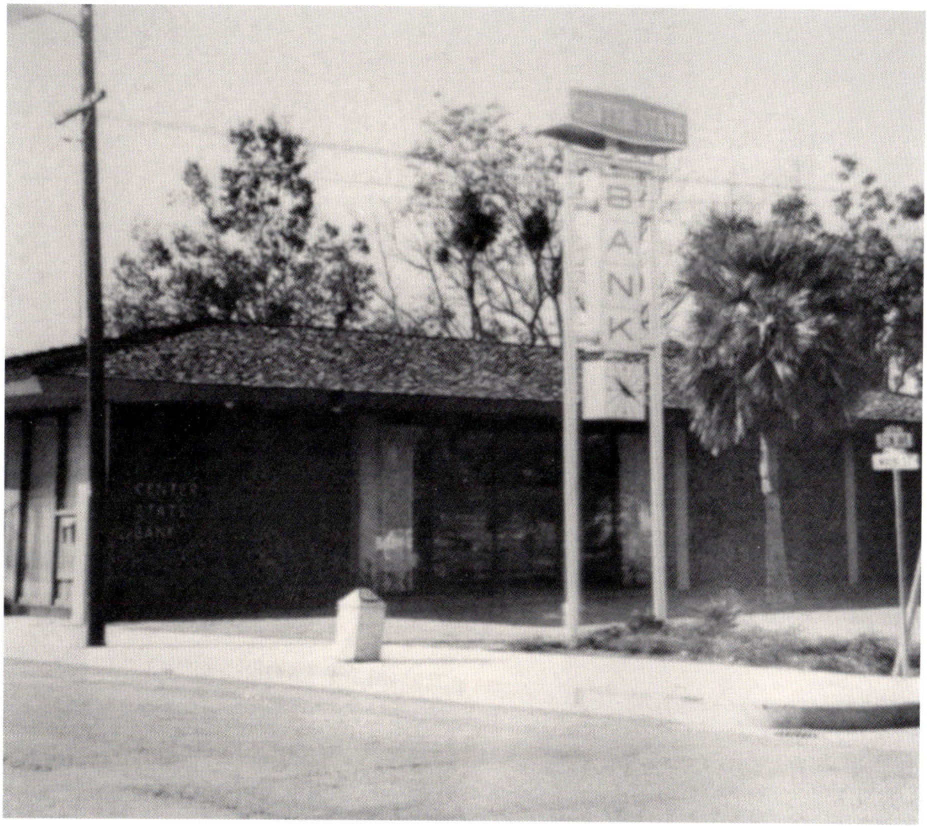

In November 1960, Ripon got a new bank—Ripon State Bank. For the next six years, it was happy at its small location at 104 W. Main Street. In 1965, with the name changed to Center State Bank, a giant leap was made to build a shiny new bank at 411 W. Main Street, just a couple of blocks down the street. In November 1987, Union Safe Deposit Bank purchased the bank. In May 2004, the bank was bought by Bank of the West and has remained as such since.

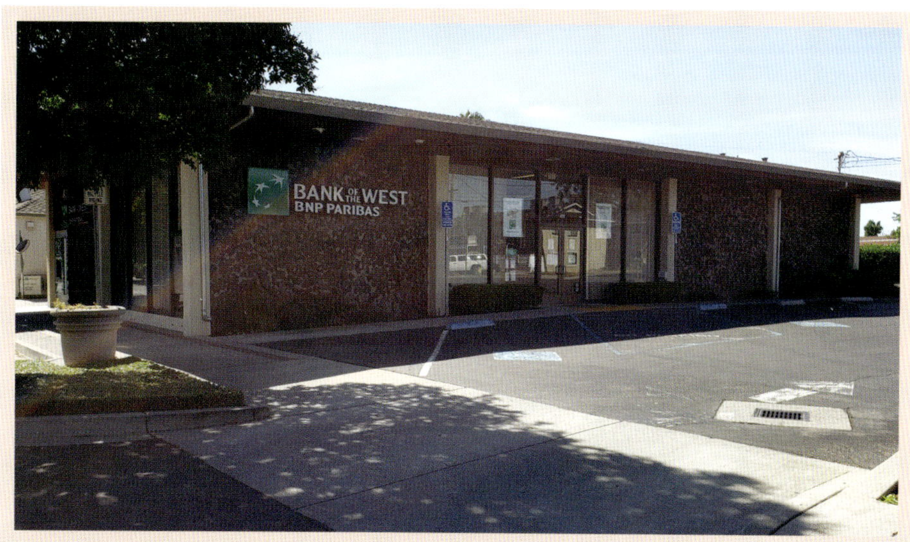

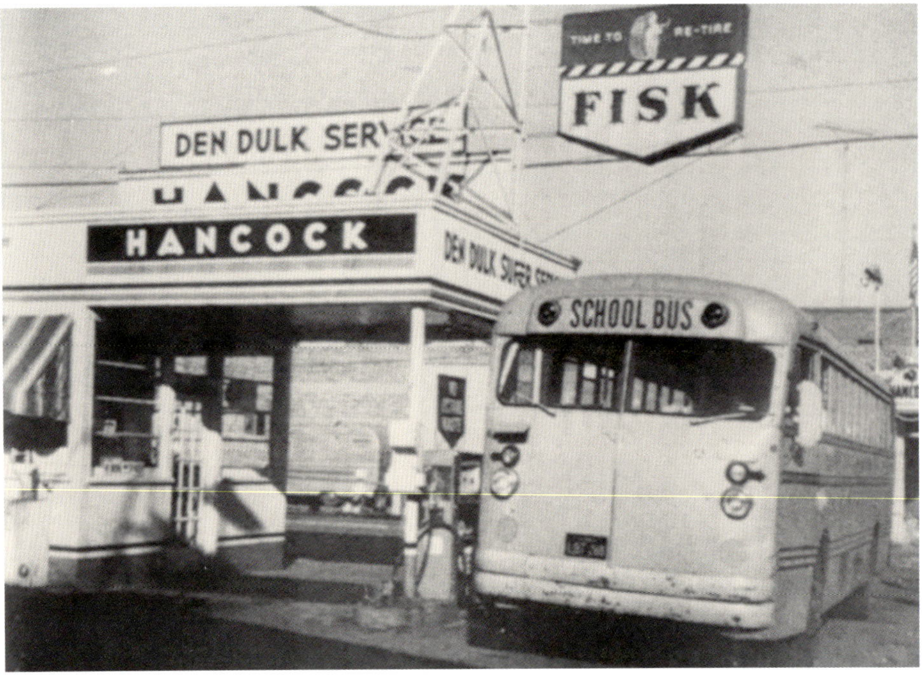

In April 1939, S.E. Vander Veen opened the Hancock gas station. In 1948, Herb Den Dulk super service took over this spot; it remained there until 1966. In February 1991, Ronald Bellew opened Valley Enterprises, specializing in car detailing and used cars. Johnny's Plumbing made use of the space for a few years, then Just Rewards occupied the small building as they worked to fulfill the trophy and ribbon needs of Ripon's citizens.

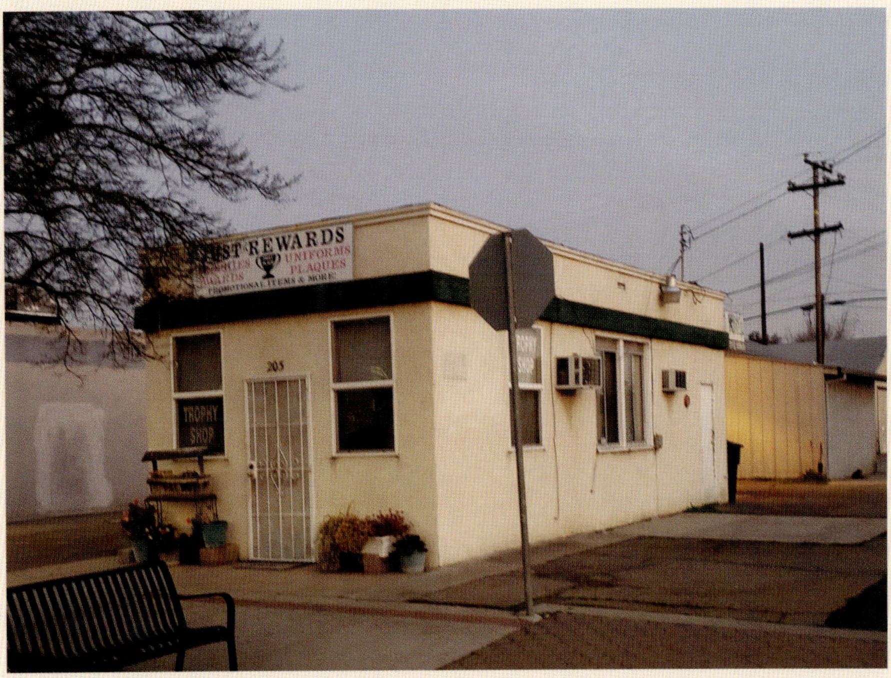

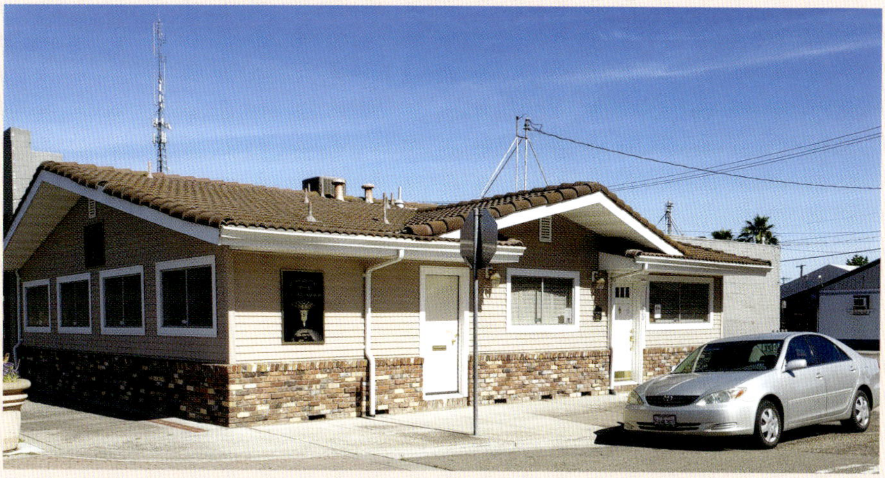

In January 1962, Dr. Marvin Seager built a brand-new 1,400-foot office in Ripon. Dr. Seager passed away unexpectedly in July 1994. Luckily for the citizens of Ripon, Dr. J. Sarkis took over the reins of the business. The building has been home to many different dentists over the years. Fortunately, it has always been a place where people could go to take care of their dental needs.

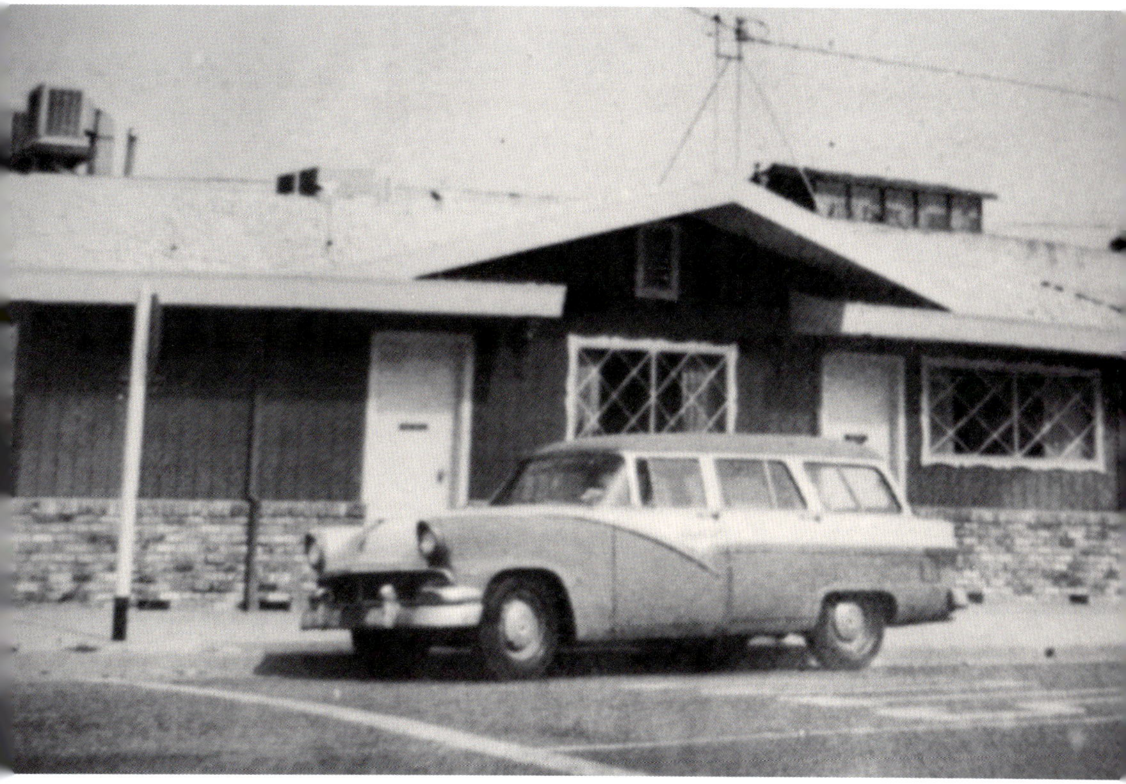

This address has been home to many businesses since this structure was built in the 1890s. Two of Ripon's pioneer families had a business here. Burt Kincaid opened the Ripon Meat Company here in 1912. Alto Van Slyke joined the company in 1918. The Kincaid and Van Slyke families continued to influence Ripon's commercial landscape for many years. In 1948, Thomas shoe shop opened, followed by Henrietta's beauty shop (1964–1981), New Impressions beauty shop (1982), and Papa Gino's pizza (1996). In recent years, it has been home to a Bible bookstore, a lingerie shop, a clothing boutique, and a wine bar.

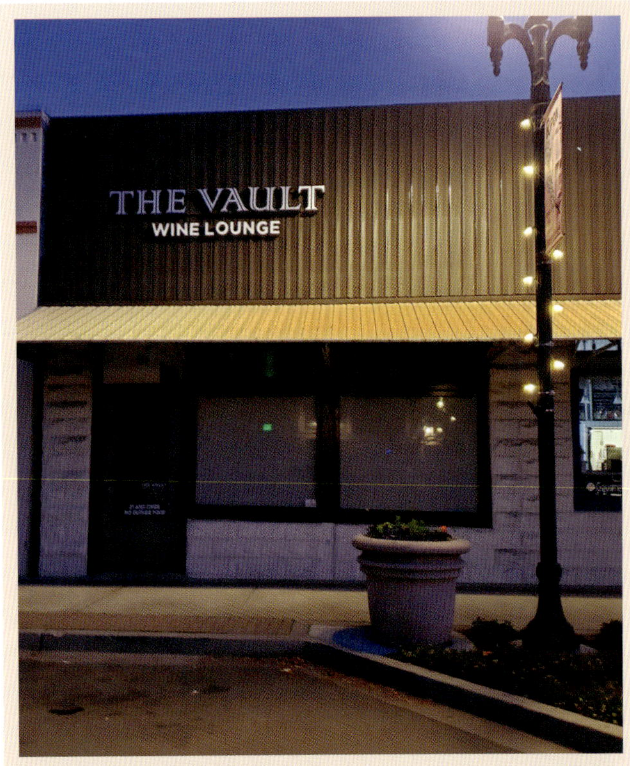

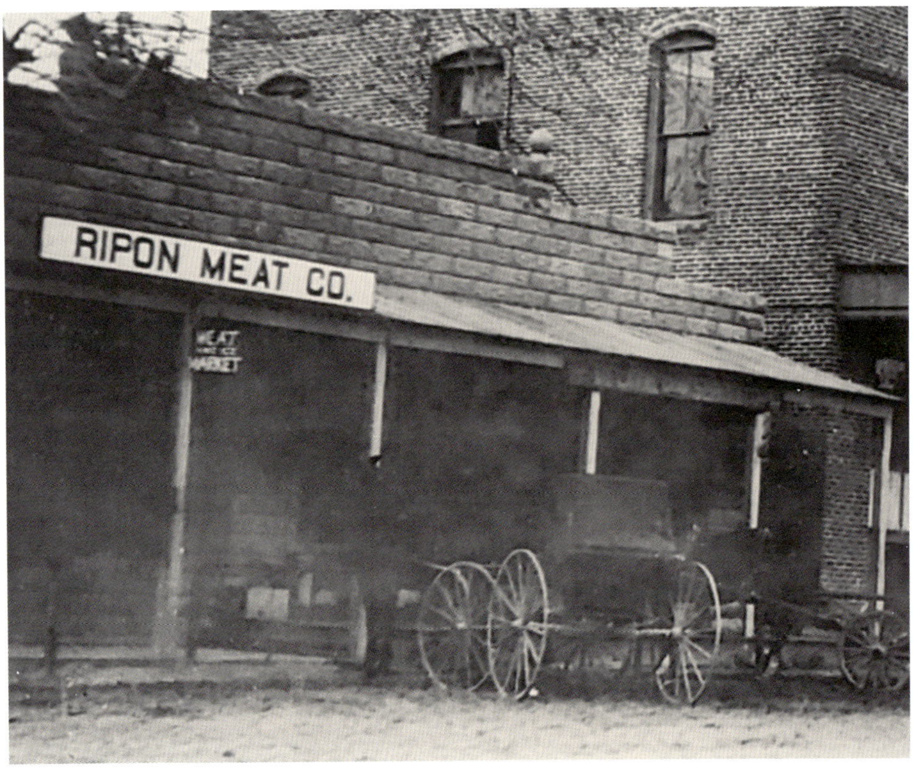

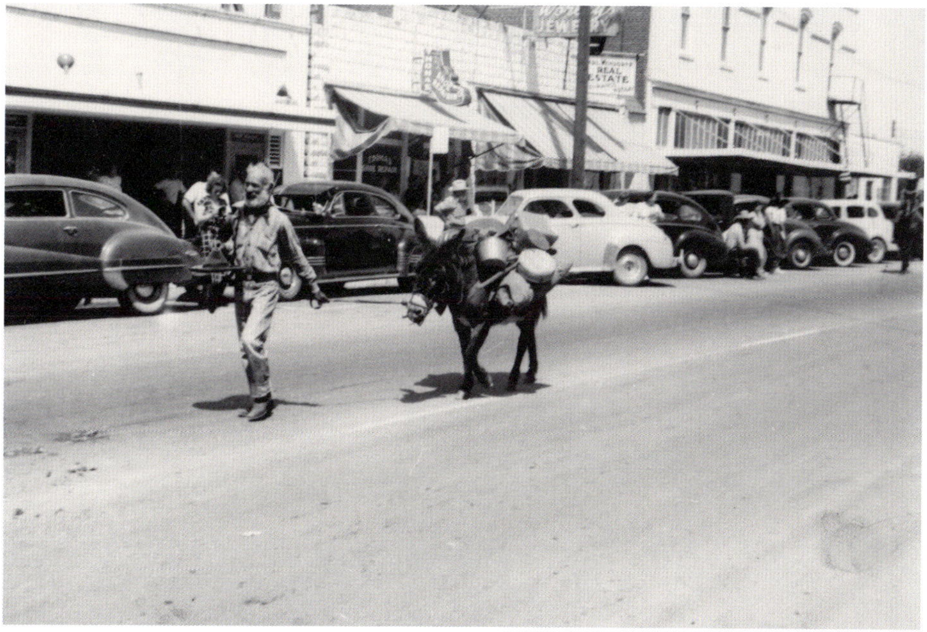

This tiny little space has an incredible history. When the Portuguese immigrants came to Ripon just after the start of the 20th century, Tony Laserde's barbershop is where they gathered. In this spot, they organized the Festa do Espirito Santo (F.D.E.S.) Ripon in 1923. In this space, Earl H. Wendorff opened his insurance company in April 1949, and Julia Grieve operated Grieve's Floral and Gift Shop from June 1951 until 1956. In February 1962, Jim Campbell started Jim's barbershop here. In August 1970, Hollis Waldon opened a laboratory. In 1981, the space went back to its roots with DyKema barbershop.

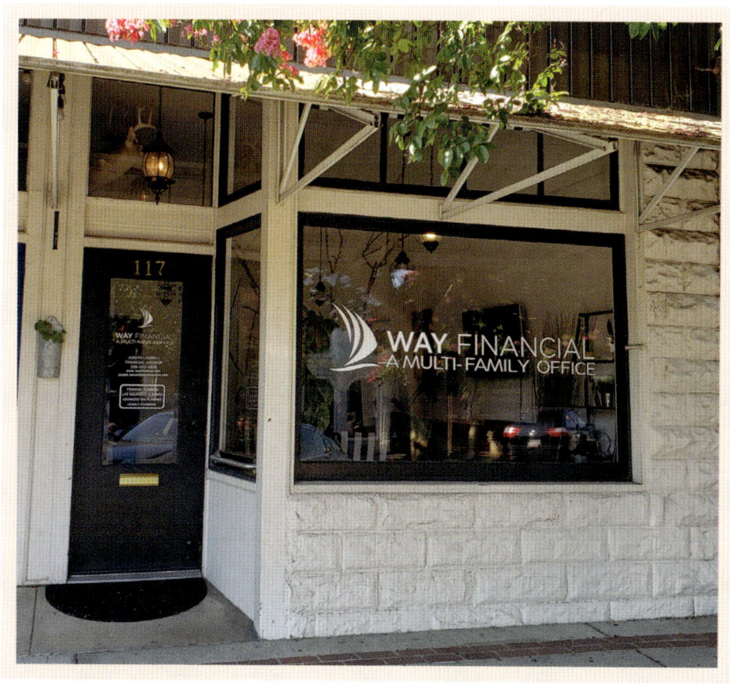

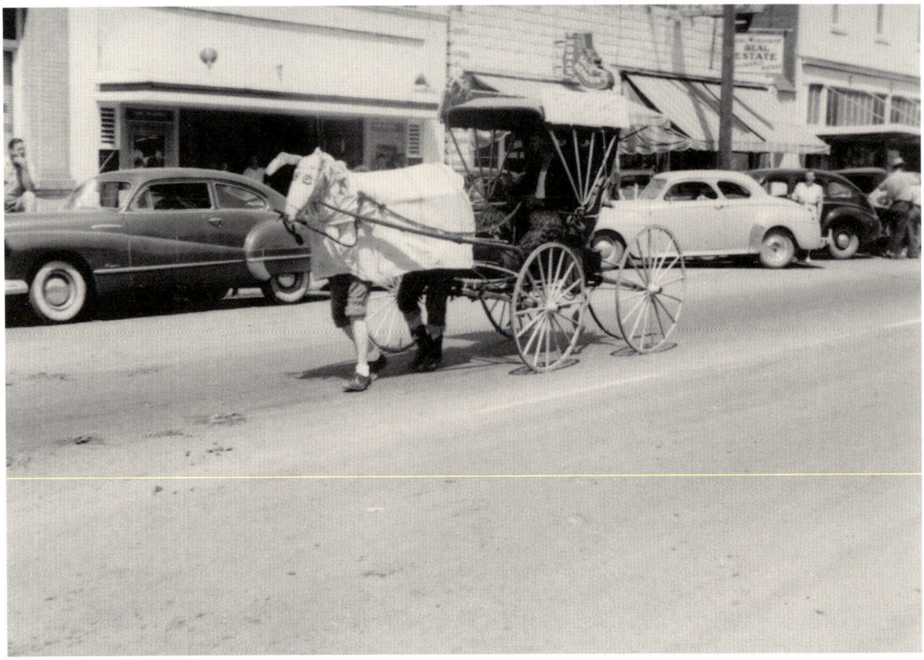

In 1920, Jake Leonardo opened Leonardo's auto service in this building, which seemed like a very strange thing to be there. In 1949, Worley's jewelry opened a store; two years later, Clarence DeBoer purchased the business and stayed there for 46 years. After DeBoer's retirement, it was a day spa, Bible bookstore, and several other businesses until it was remodeled into a small restaurant.

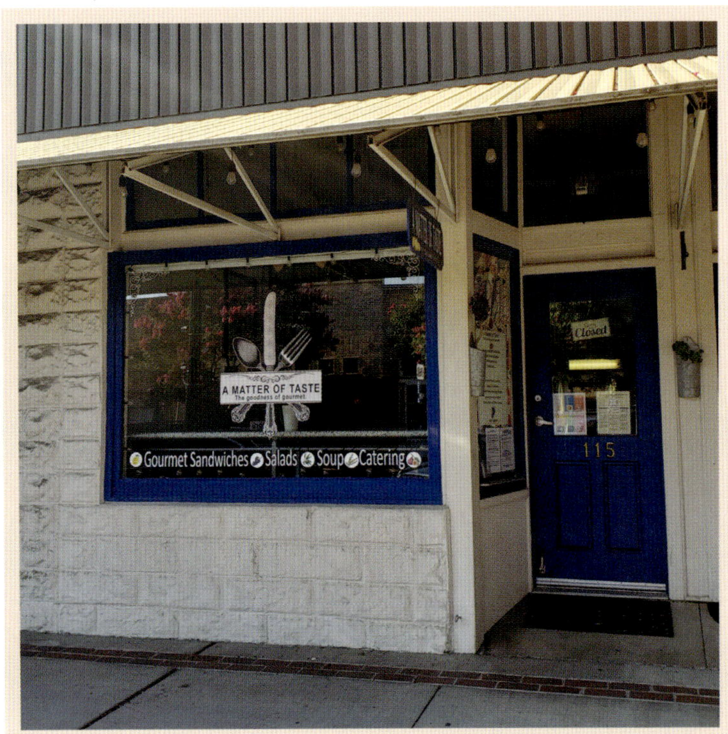

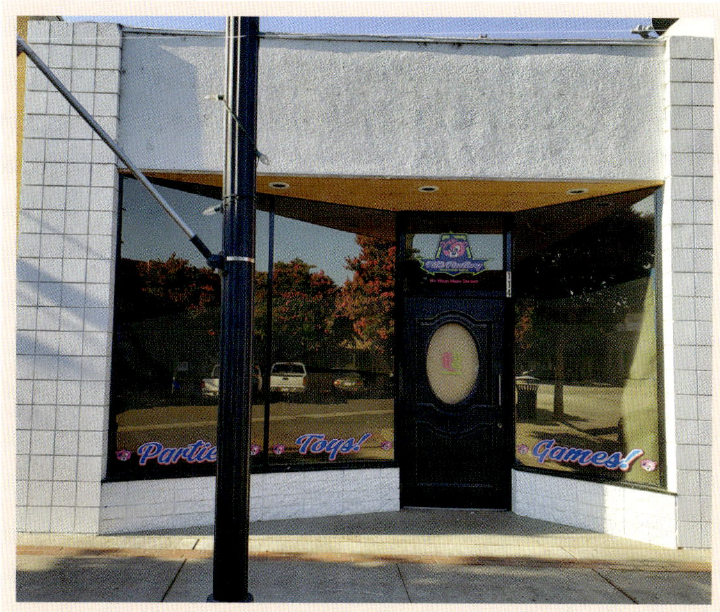

In June 1962, the city was ready for a business that catered to the men in the community. John Hoff and Arvin Boersma opened a men's clothing store called Jon and Arv's menswear. The shop carried everything that a well-dressed man needed. In 1965, the men went back to farming. In October 1982, "looking good" was replaced with "seeing good" when Duane Kirk opened Almond Blossom Optometry; in February 1987, he needed more space. In February 1989, Michelle Ioppini opened Secret Garden Floral. This space has seen the birth of many businesses.

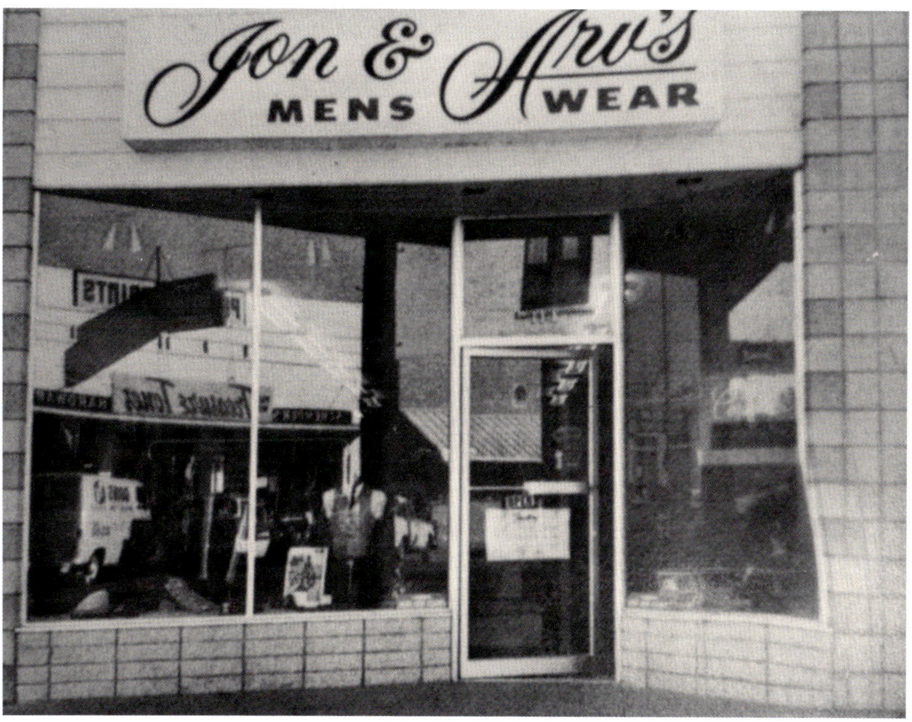

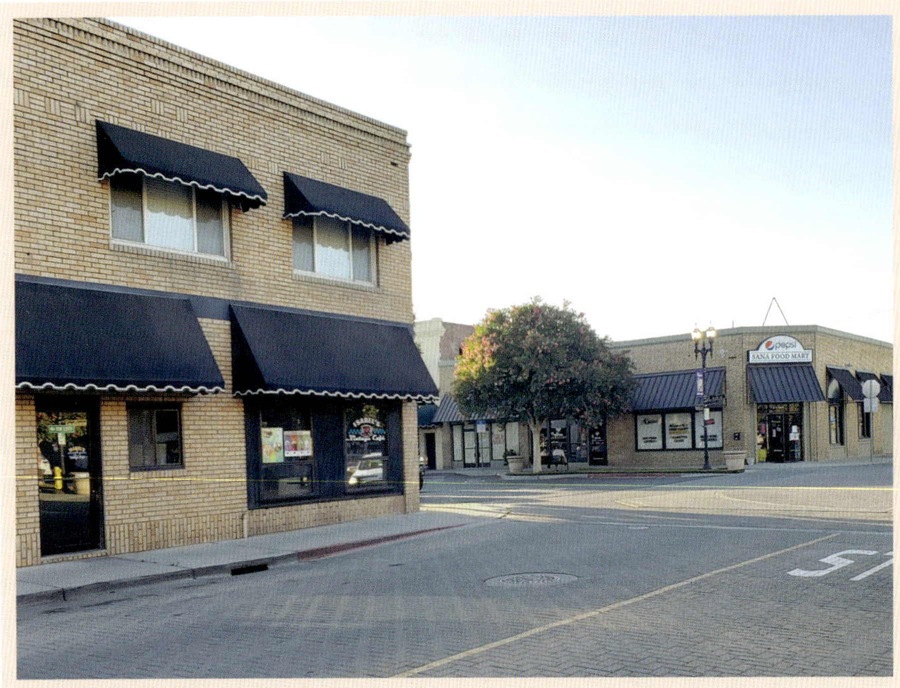

This 1950s photograph was taken by Stanley Fulton at the corner of Stockton and Main Streets. Paul Ness built the Ripon Drug building (on the right) in the 1920s. Heine Spaman operated the Red and White market across the street. This building was initially constructed in 1921 as the First National Bank. The drugstore moved to new quarters in 1965. These two prominent buildings have had many lives as different types of businesses. Now, the drugstore is a small restaurant, and the bank building is once again a market.

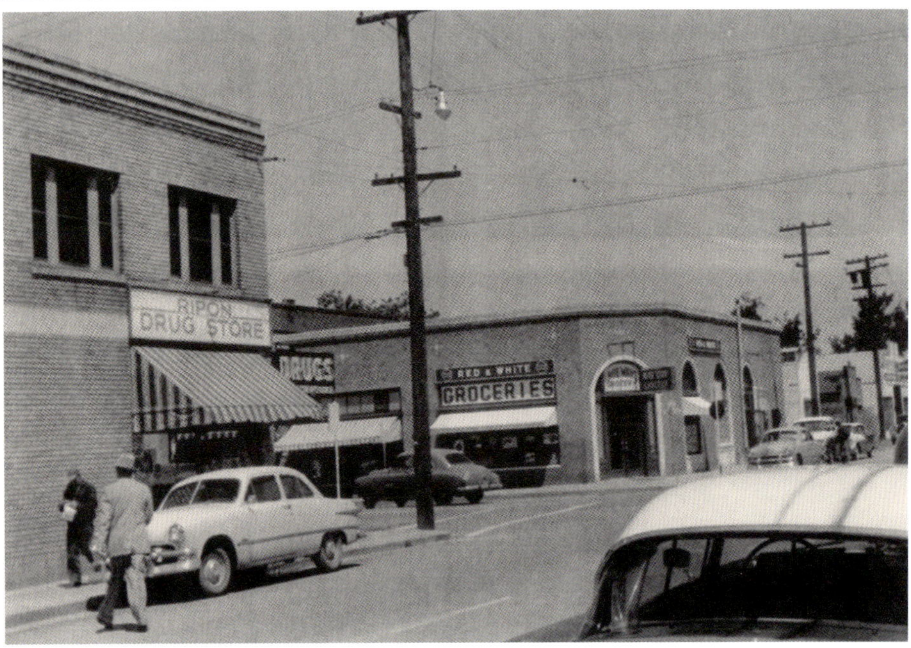

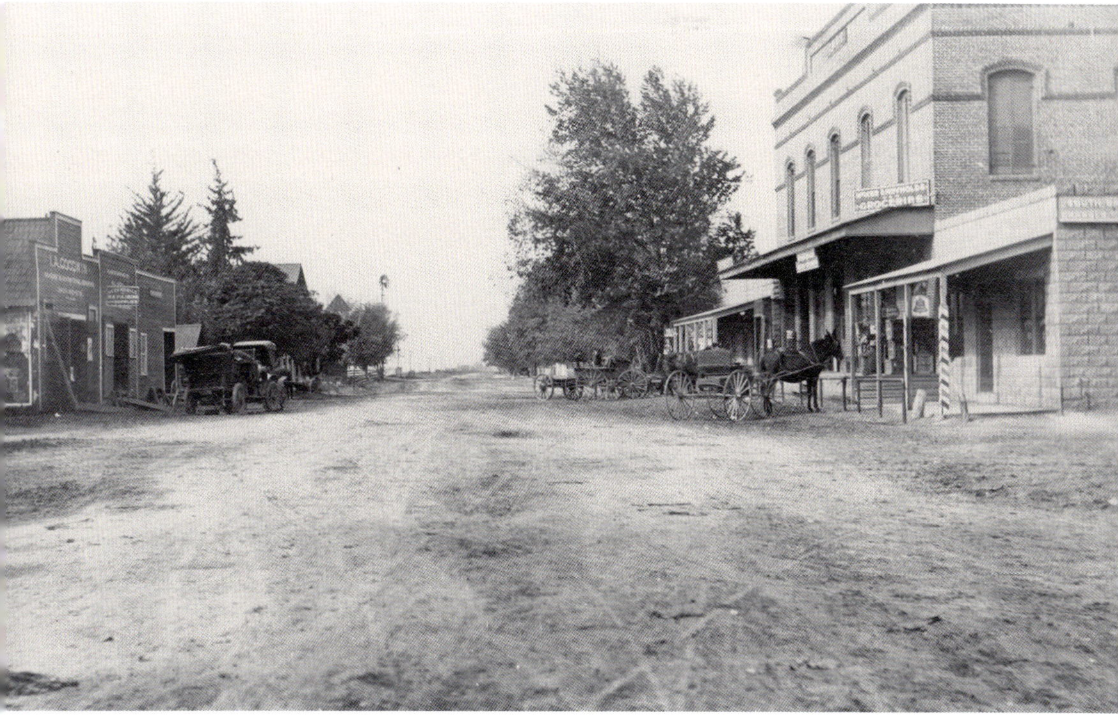

This view, looking north, is probably one of the most photographed sections of Main Street. The structure on the right is the Odd Fellows building, which was erected in 1886. North of the Odd Fellows building, the white block buildings were erected in the early 1890s and served as the retail district of Ripon. The small-block building to the south of the Odd Fellows building was constructed around 1895. On the left is Irvin Goodwin's blacksmith and auto-repair business.

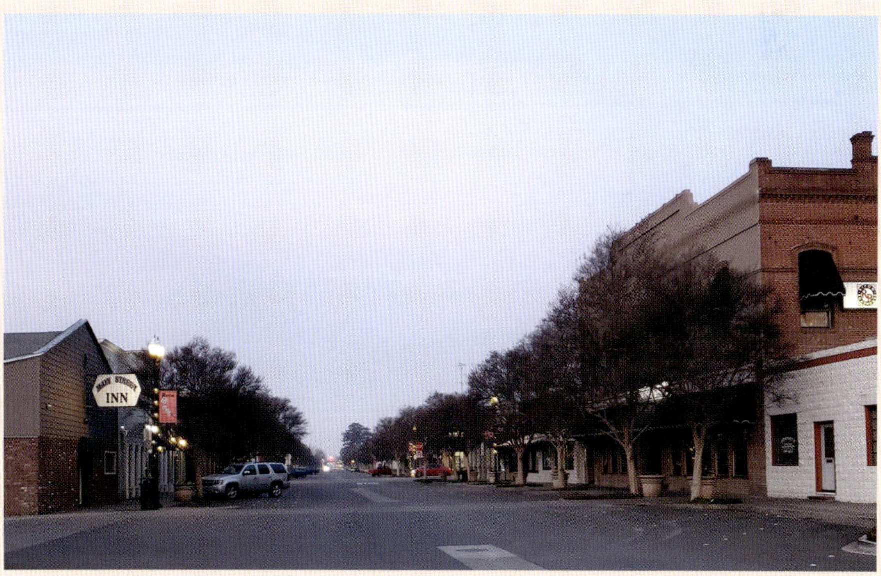

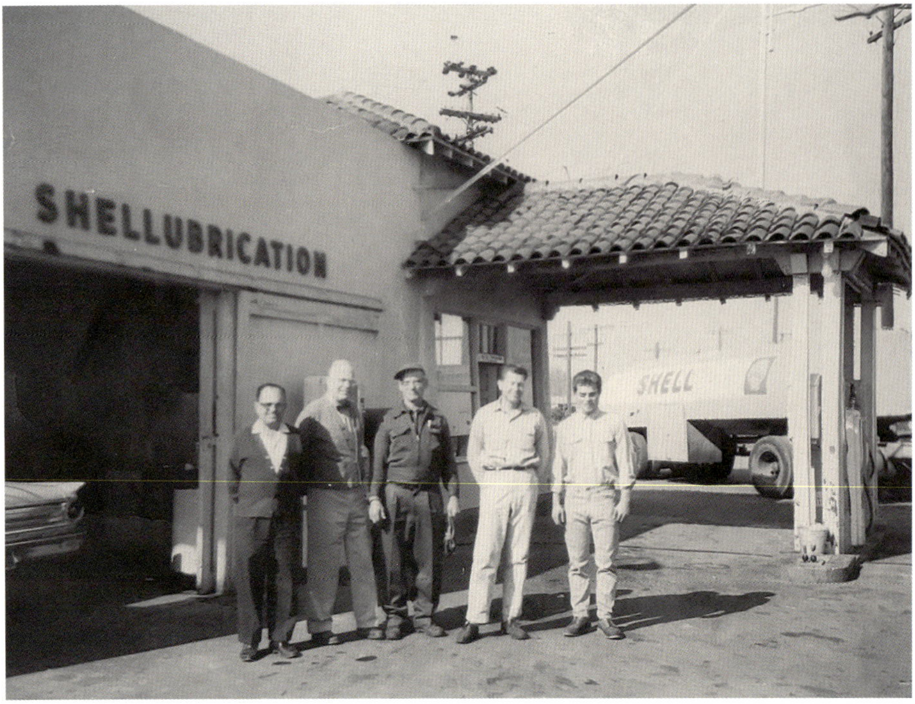

The patriarch of the Thiemann family, John Thiemann, moved from New York to Ripon in 1922. That same year, John became a partner in the Ripon Service Station. Just two years later, in 1924, a Spanish-style station was built. In 1926, John owned the station. John's son Jerry worked for his dad when he was in high school. Jerry became more involved with the business after graduating in 1947, and things were going well then. In 1963, Caltrans decided to widen the freeway through the city. (Past image courtesy of the Thiemann family.)

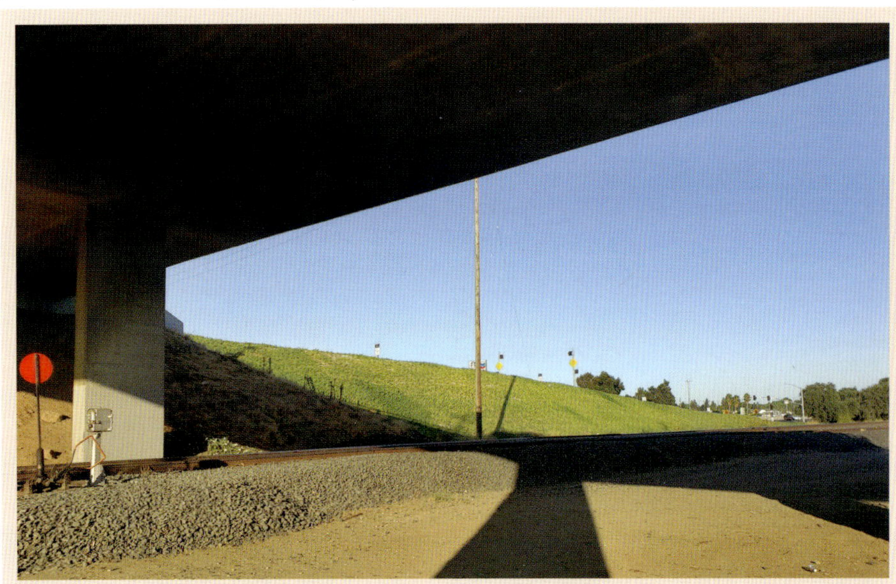

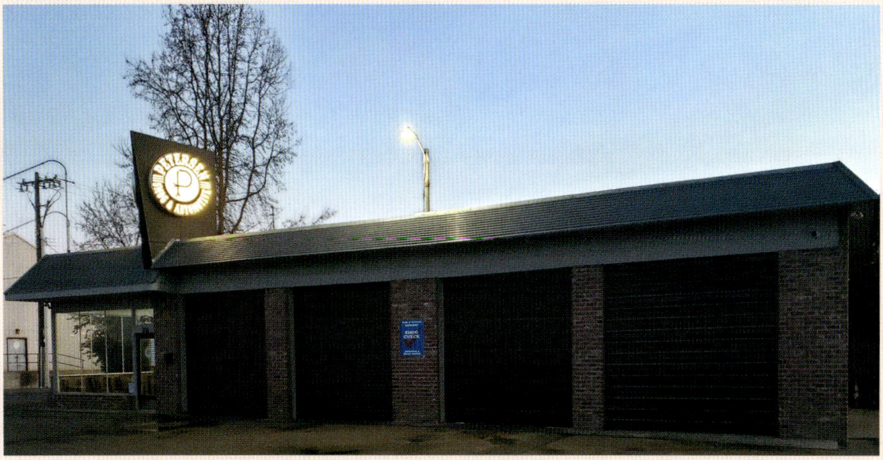

The iconic Spanish-style building shown here has since been torn down, and an on-ramp to the freeway has taken its place. Jerry Thiemann, being an astute businessman, found a gas station being demolished and paid just $5 for the building; however, it had to be moved to Ripon and remodeled, which cost an additional $5,000. In 1986, Jerry's son Steve took over the business, turning it into a smog-examination station. Now, the station is seeing a new page in its life thanks to current owners Leland and Amy Petersen. (Past image courtesy of the Thiemann family.)

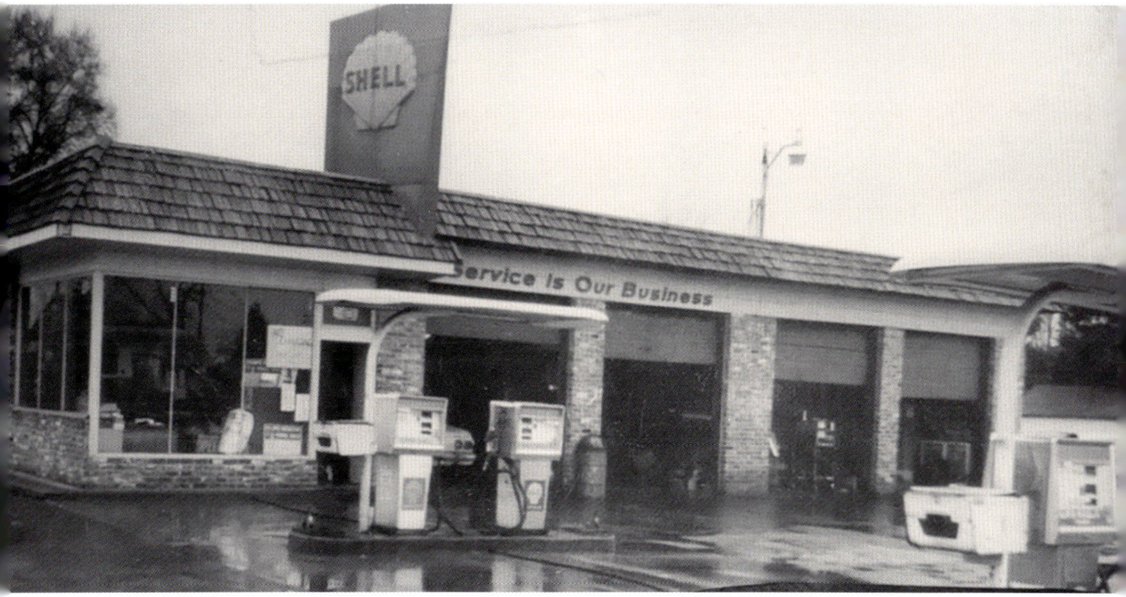

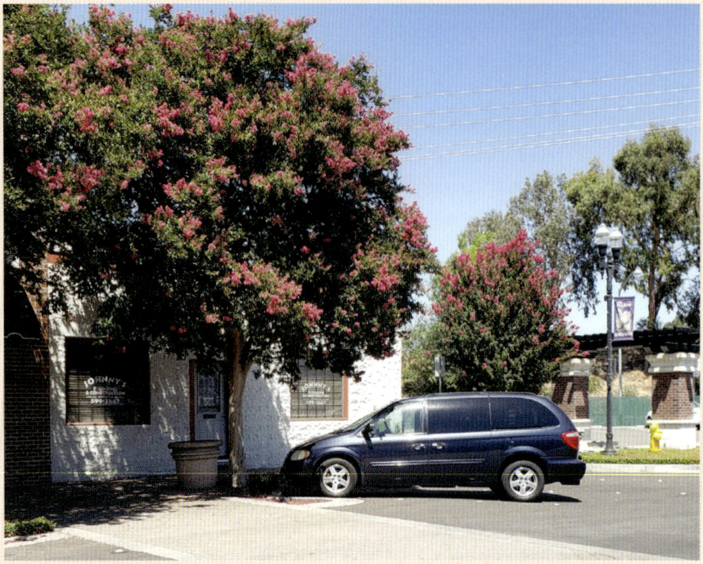

This is the Bodeson Stage Line. The stage picked up riders in front of the post office and transported them to Stockton for 50¢. Francis Lewis Bodeson arrived in Ripon in 1887 and tried farming but was unsuccessful. In 1904, he was appointed the first rural mail carrier, with his horse-drawn wagon covering 24 miles. In 1916, he passed the mail service on to his son and started a stage line, real estate office, and Farmers Mutual Insurance office. All of this incredible history took place at this building.

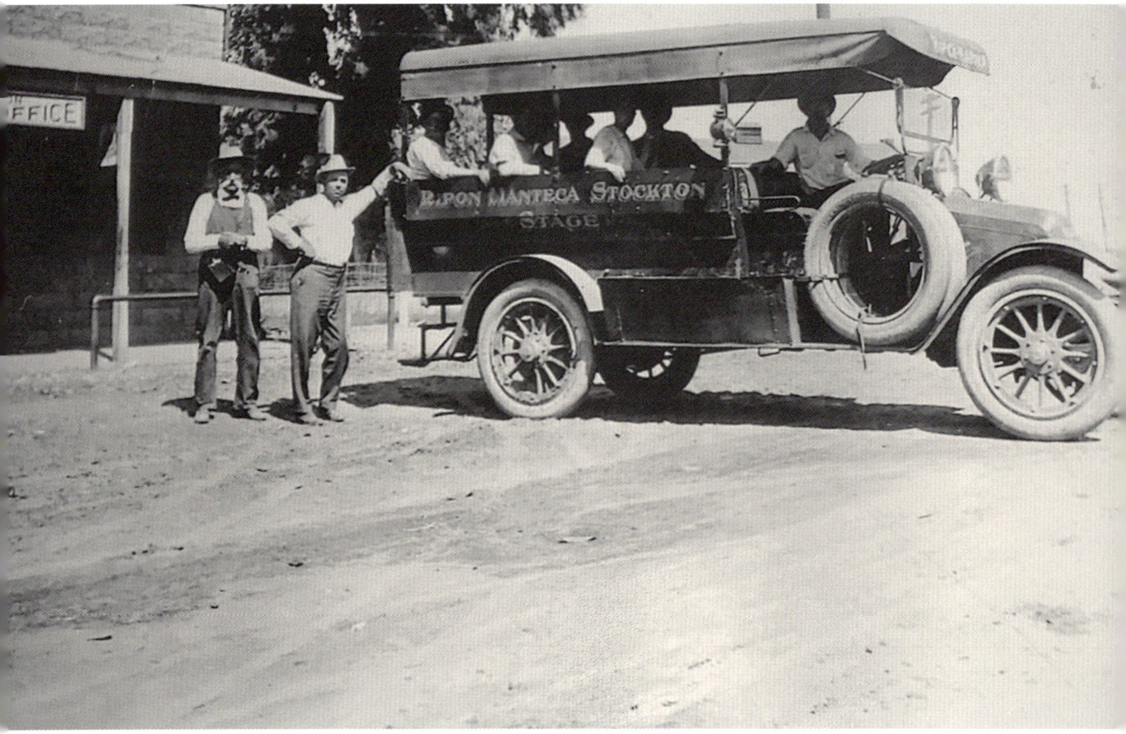

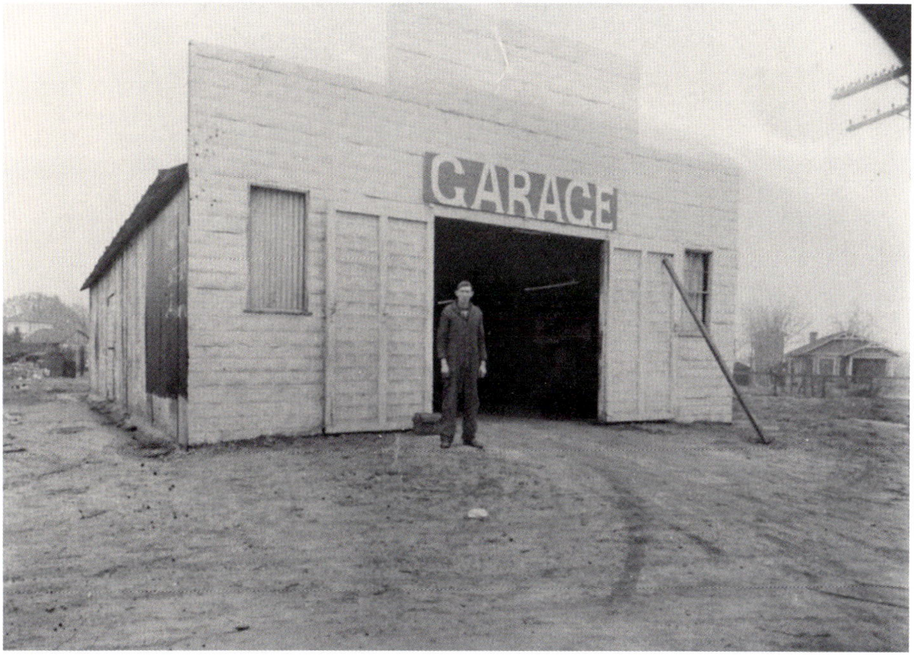

This 1934 image shows Walter Swier standing in front of his garage. In 1946, Ed and John Swier had returned from the war effort and joined Walter in the business. Walter had been in the gas station business, so he figured he could also sell the cars that use the gas; thus began the Swier & Son Studebaker automobile dealership. In 1954, Walter retired. In 1984, his grandson Roger took over the business. Roger has now handed it over to his son Daniel, and the legacy continues.

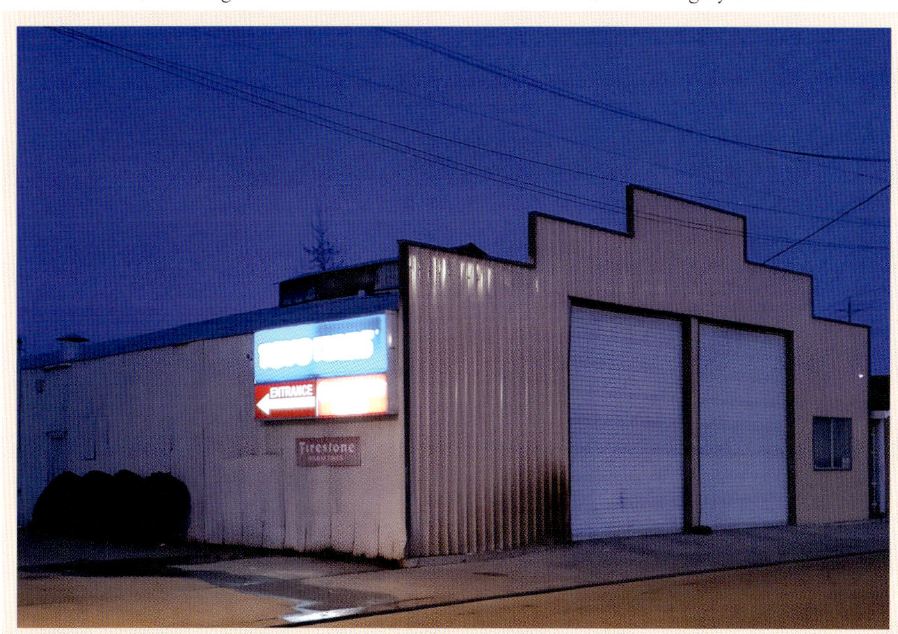

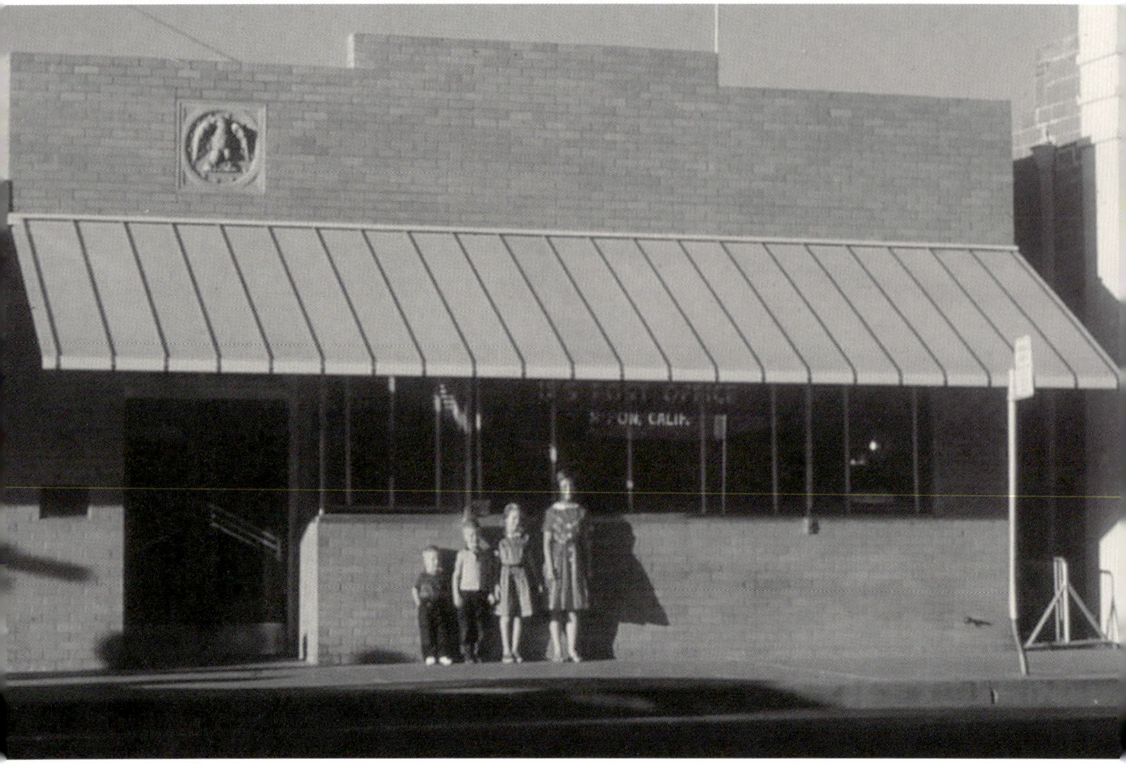

The Ripon post office opened in this new building in June 1950. George Markham had started the project, and it became one of the last buildings that he would erect. Sadly, Markham passed away in November 1949, never to see this structure completed. In this 1950s photograph are, from left to right, assistant postmaster Bert Huber's children Jeff, John, Judy, and Jeanne, who were possibly visiting their dad at work. In 1989, when the post office moved to new quarters for the fifth time, the building was remodeled and repurposed. (Past image courtesy of the Huber family.)

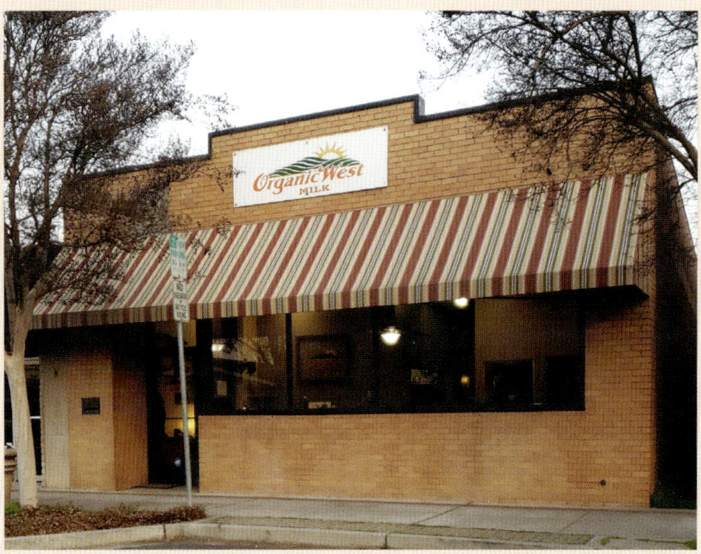

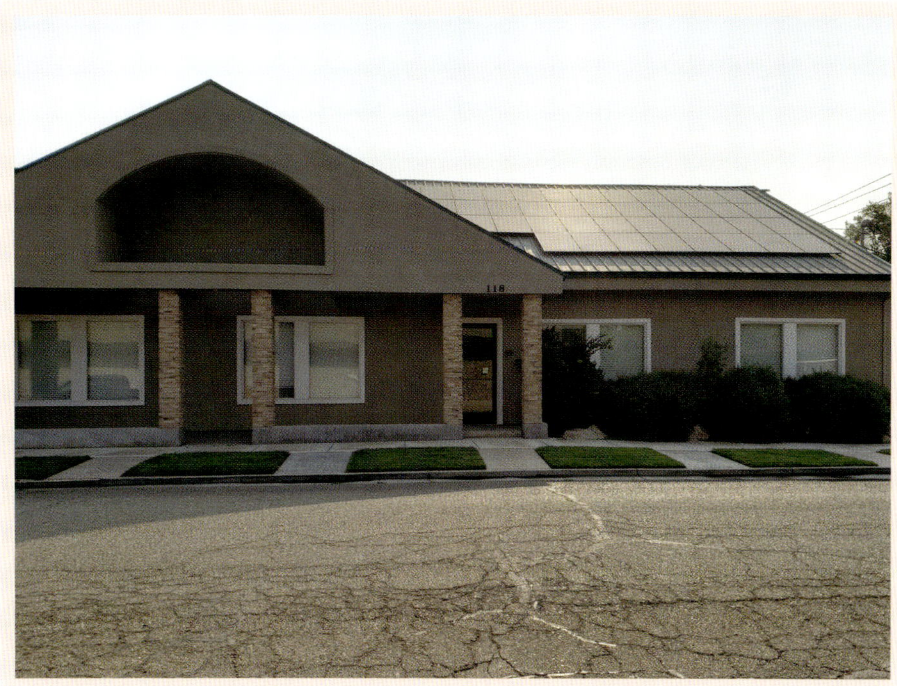

This 1950s photograph shows the fun of an Easter egg hunt in downtown Ripon. The building in the background is Harry's Garage on South Elm Street. It served the business well from the 1950s until 1964, when it moved to new quarters on Walnut Street. Schemper's hardware took over the space and remained there for many years until it also moved. Then, the building was bought and extensively remodeled for the new owners, Duct Testers. The empty field in the past image is where the Ripon drugstore would later be built. (Past image courtesy of the Huber family.)

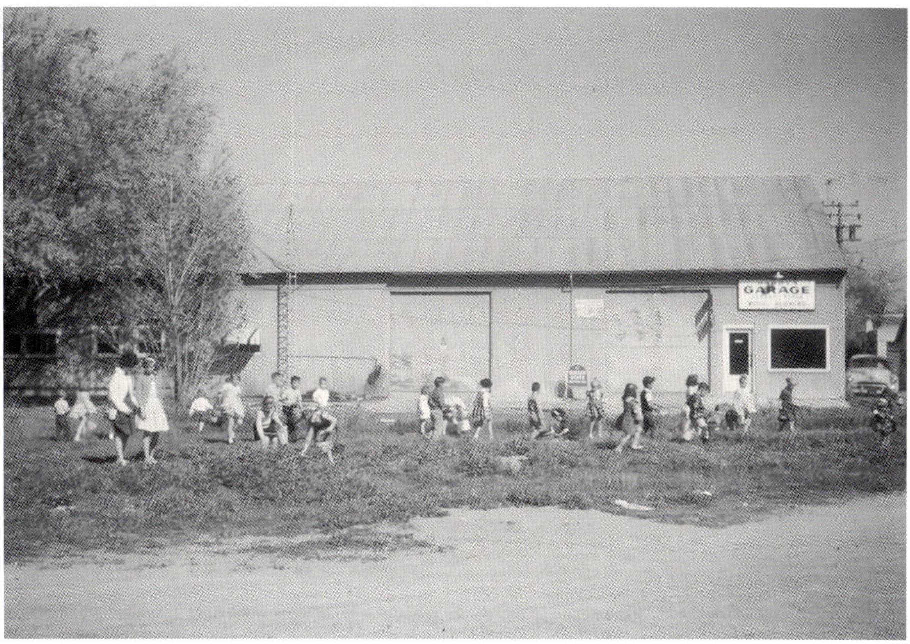

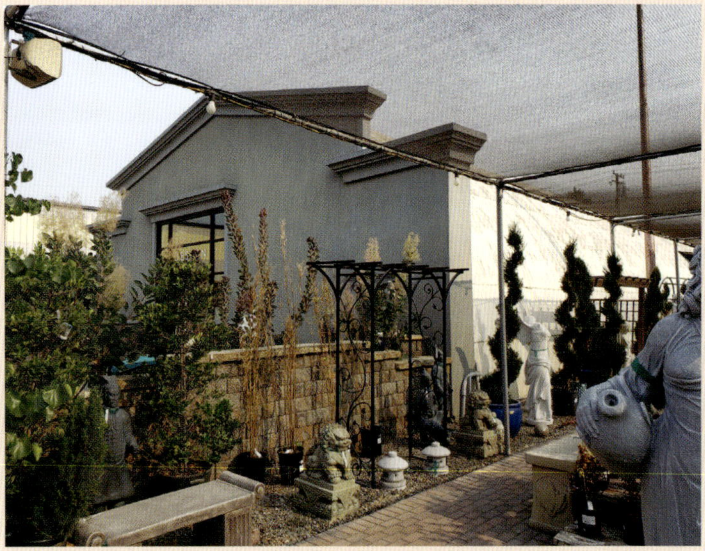

The people of Ripon hated to waste anything, including buildings. This 1962 photograph shows the Quonset-style building that was Douma's market as it was being moved. It was repurposed at its new home at what was the Meyenberg milk plant. After the plant closed, the building was utilized for an assortment of other uses. Now, the building is being used as a design center at the complex, which also houses a nursery.

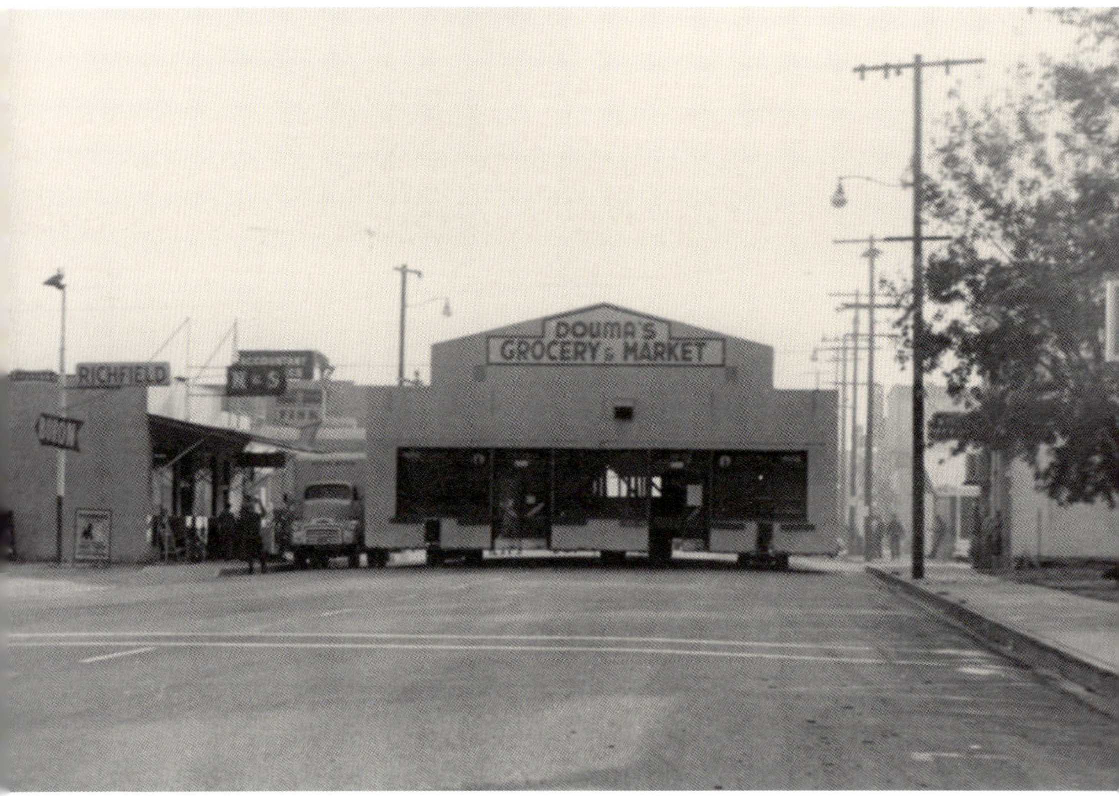

CHAPTER 2

Home Is Where the Heart Is

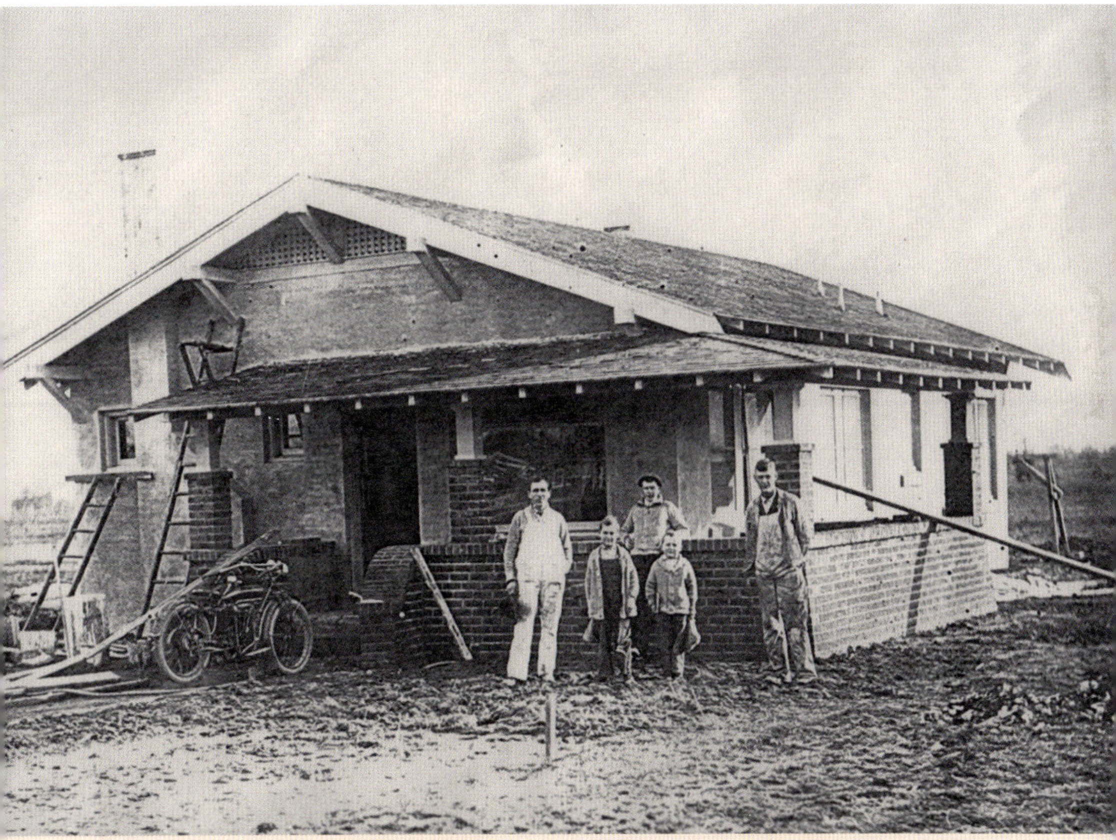

Often, homes are seen as simply the brick and mortar they are constructed with. But when the cobwebs of time are wiped away, it is clear they are made of the celebrations of life. Family gatherings are the puzzle pieces that have made the community the place that people have chosen to live in. This chapter shows how these homes and their families have shaped the Ripon community.

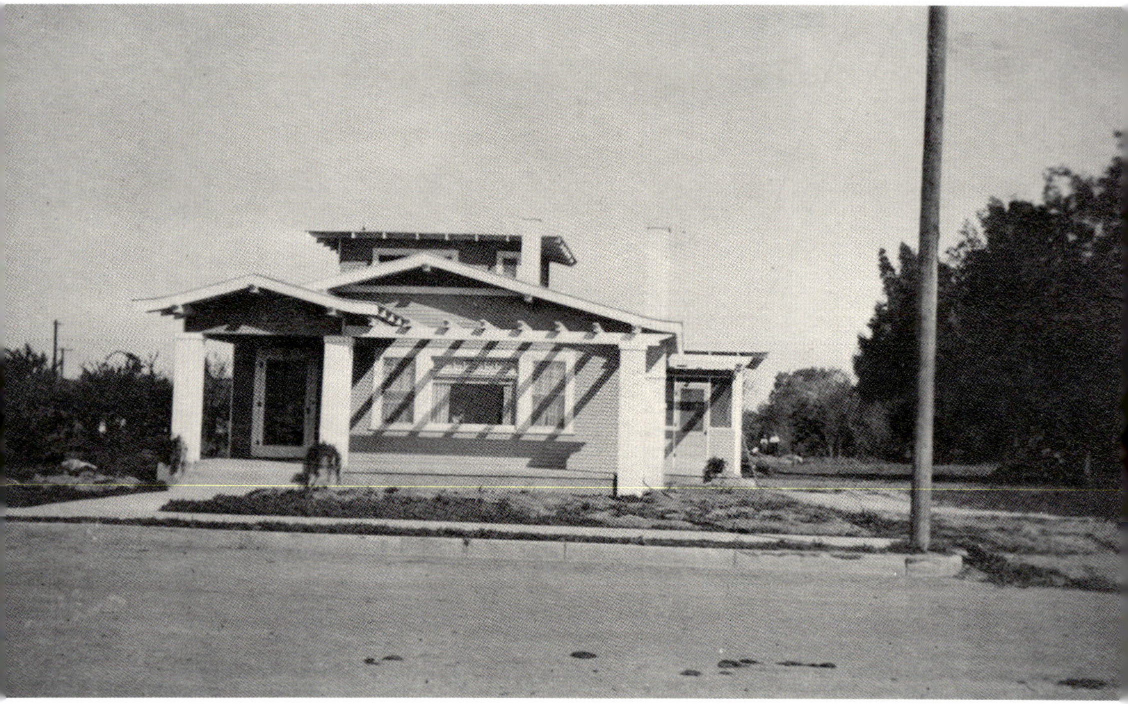

In April 1918, Rev. J.J. Kelly of the First Congregational Church sold two lots near the church to J.H. Capps. In May 1918, John Madsen was hired as the contractor and finished the foundation, and in June 1918, this home was nearing completion. The home has housed many families since then. In 1968, Sherman Verver purchased the home for his new wife, Gert; they started their life and raised a family here. In 1984, Main Street Floral moved in, and it remained in business for 20 years. Now, the home is used for a pet grooming business.

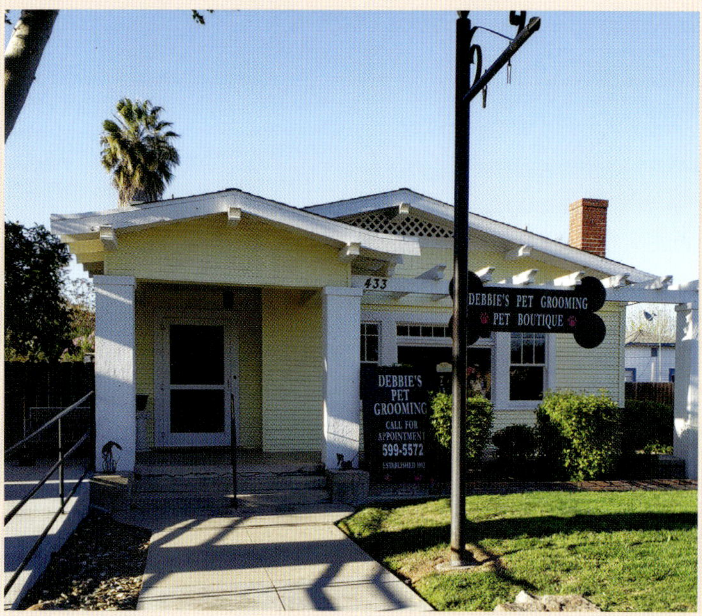

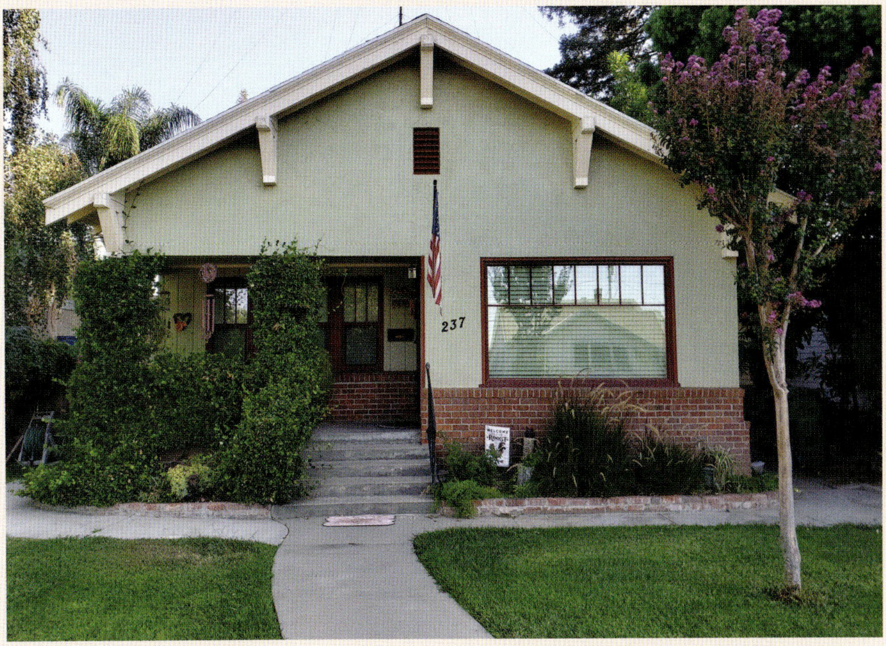

The Andrew Douma residence on Second Street is pictured here with the Douma family. The Doumas, who arrived in Ripon on November 10, 1918, probably were some of the most giving individuals who made a lasting effect on Ripon. The home has gone through some remodeling, and now the front porch is part of the main home. Vernon (Douma) Weidert lived in the house with her husband until they passed away. (Past image courtesy of Ripon Historical Society.)

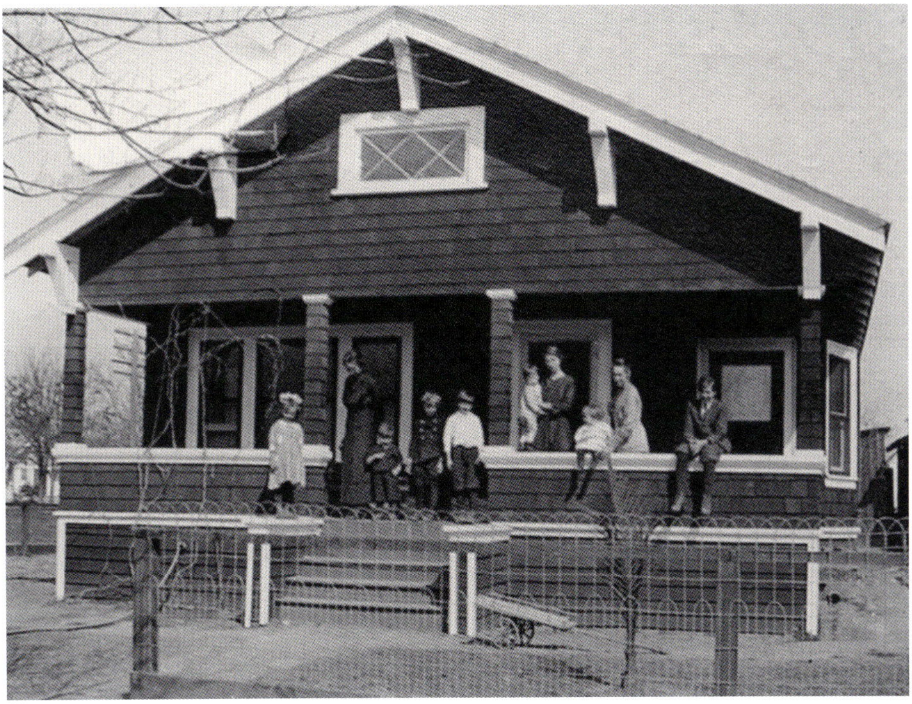

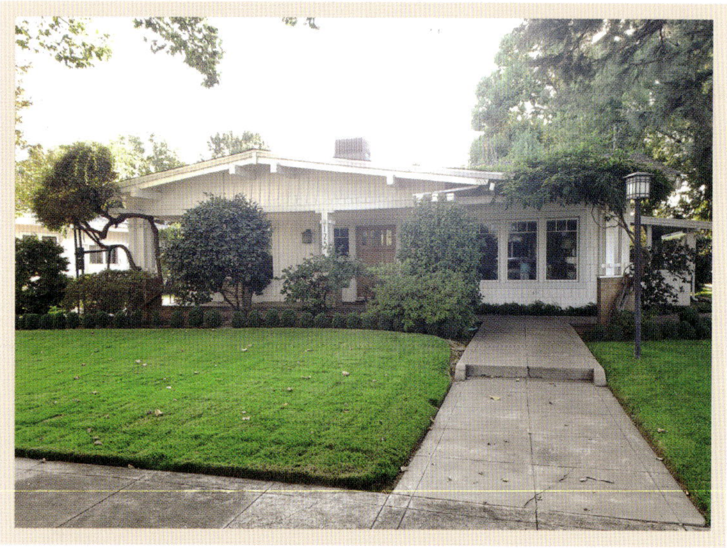

This home was built in 1911 for Dr. Chapella. In 1913, it was sold to Dr. Ned B. Gould and his family. Dr. Gould also owned the two lots next to his home; those were used for tennis courts, as tennis was very popular in Ripon. Alie Quatrel, a farmer and nationally ranked tennis player in 1912, would often join J. Verne Brainard Brown and Dr. Ned Gould, along with two bankers, Tom Smethers and Huge Leavitt Dickey, to play tennis. After the Ripon Hospital burned down in 1926, Dr. Gould moved his practice to Modesto and started the Gould Medical Center. (Past image courtesy of LuAnn Vander Meulen.)

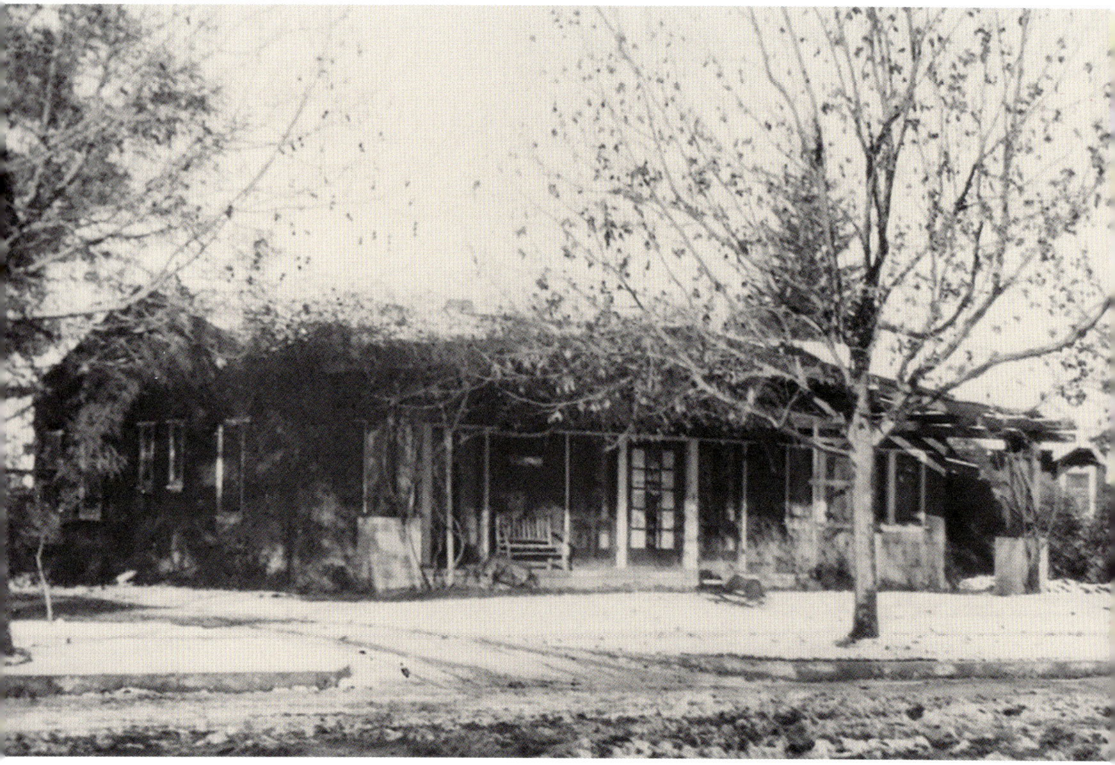

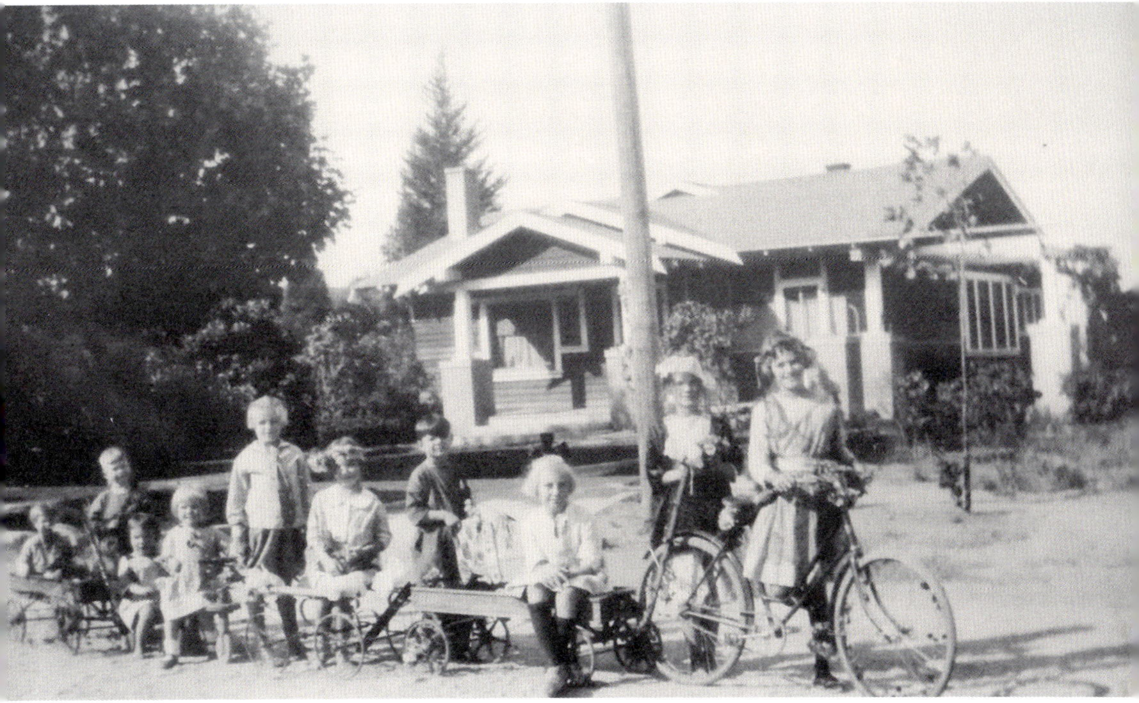

In 1921, J. Verne Brainard and Ruth Brown arrived in Ripon. Verne and Ruth were teachers, and soon, Verne became a principal—a position he held until 1931. This vintage photograph features what was referred to as "the Orange Street gang." Some of the youngsters in the image are the Brown children (Phyllis, Molly, Cary, and Connie) and Jeanette Gould, the daughter of Dr. Ned B. Gould, the Browns' neighbor. In this early-1920s image, the children had decided that it was time for a Fourth of July parade, and thus began a tradition. (Past image courtesy of the Brown family.)

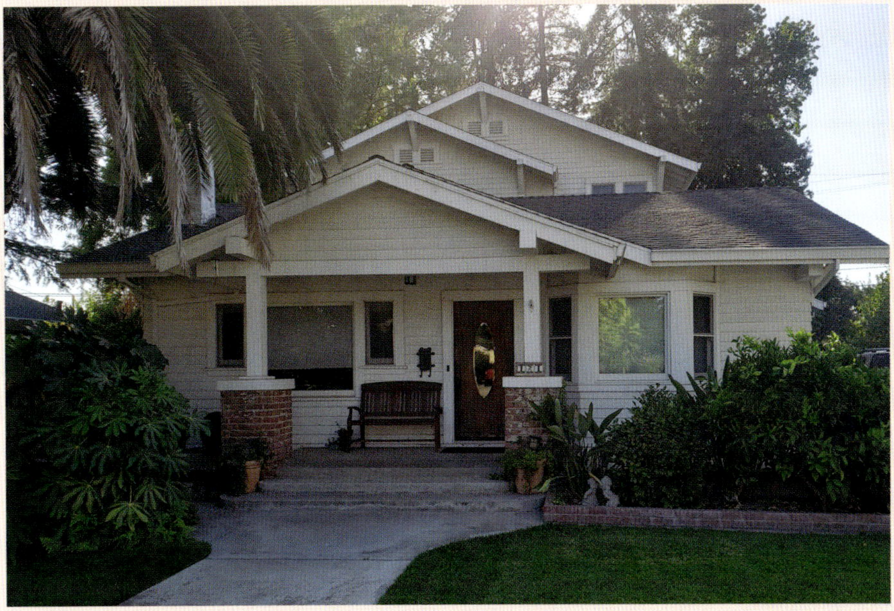

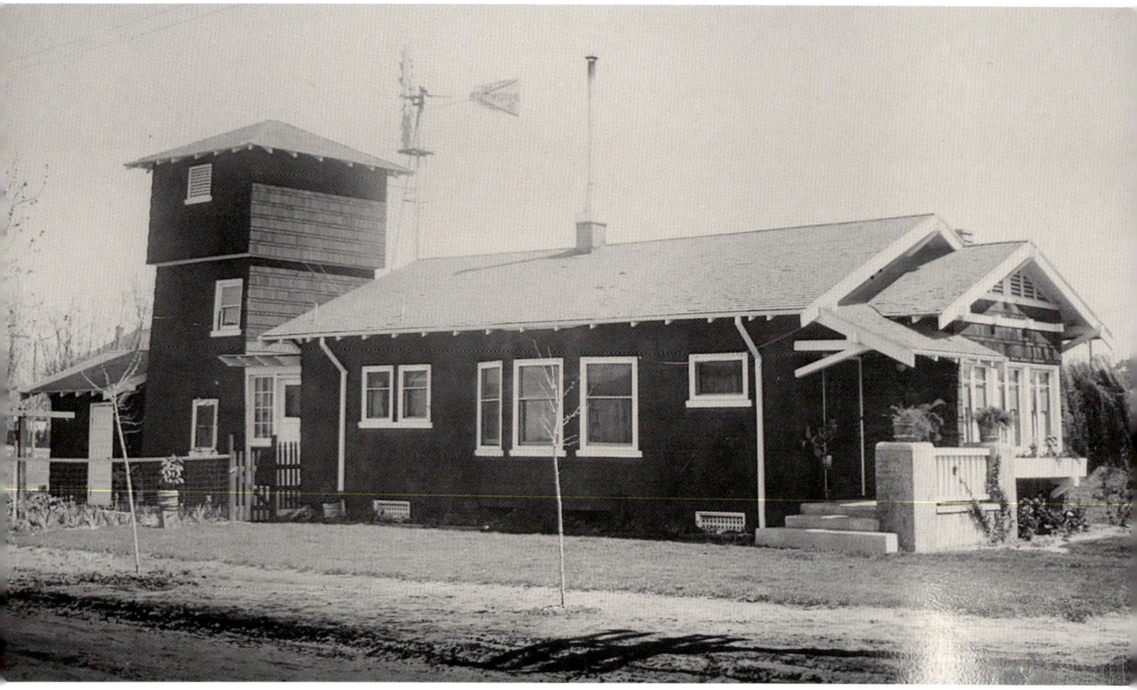

This beautiful home first entered the limelight in Ripon when Charlie McBrian moved there in 1912. McBrian was an attorney who moved from Oklahoma to Ripon after doing well in land development. The local newspaper, the *Ripon Record*, was started by McBrian and his partner A.J. Snow. The home's next major change came when Eunice Decker moved here in the 1980s and opened the Tank House Gift Shop. In 2004, Al and Helen Caetano took over running the successful gift shop and stewarding the care of the majestic home.

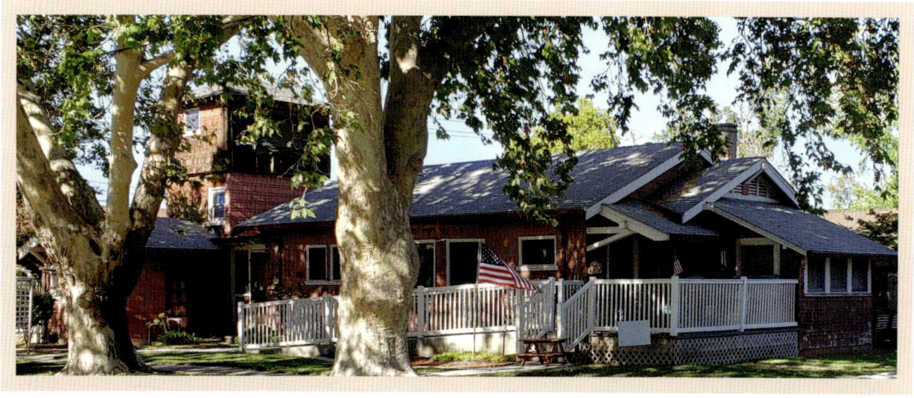

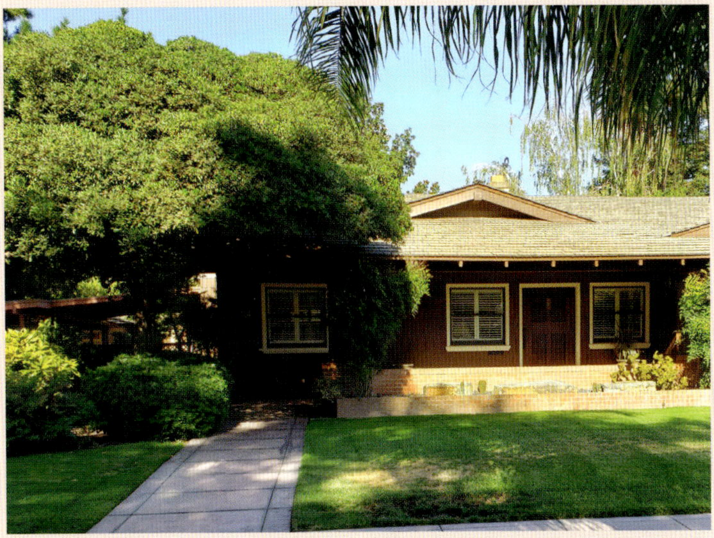

Judge Sidney Reynolds was a partner in McKee and Reynolds Mercantile in Ripon. This home was started in 1913 by Reynolds for his new wife, Byrd. He hired six carpenters to complete it quickly. Sidney carved out two lots in his orchard for the home, and the back of the house still has a carriage house and stable. Sidney passed in March 1954; the home was occupied by his wife until 1960. That is when Arthur and Henrietta Clemens purchased this house, and it is still in the Clemens family today. (Past image courtesy of Arthur Clemens.)

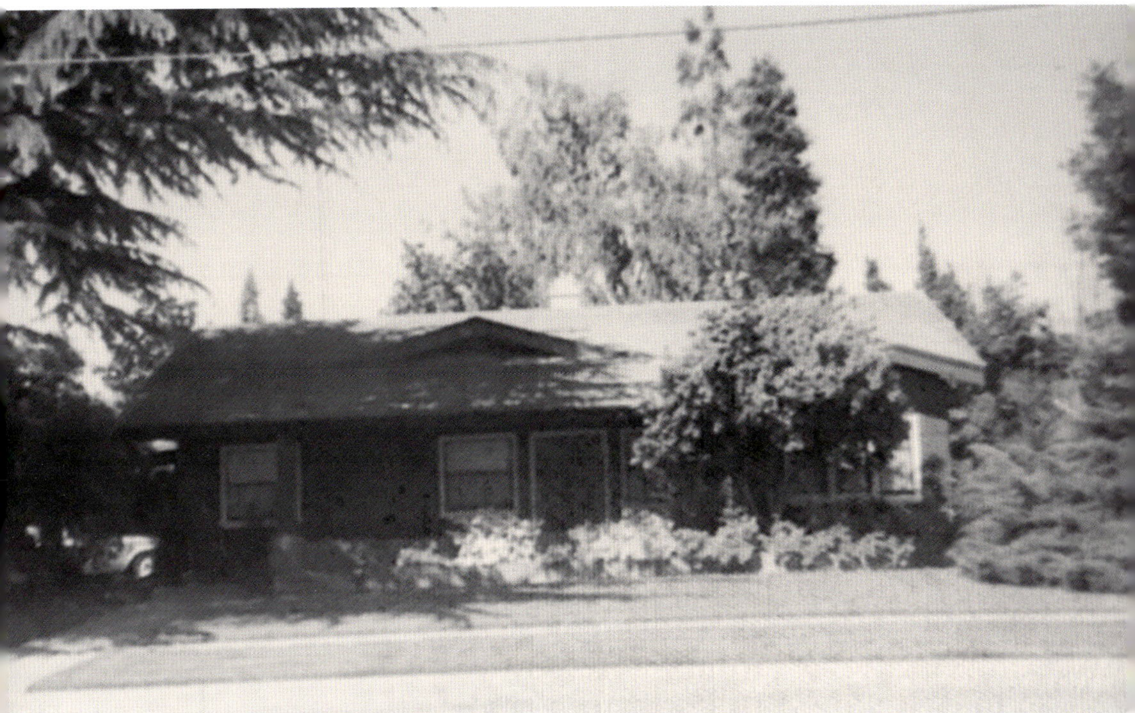

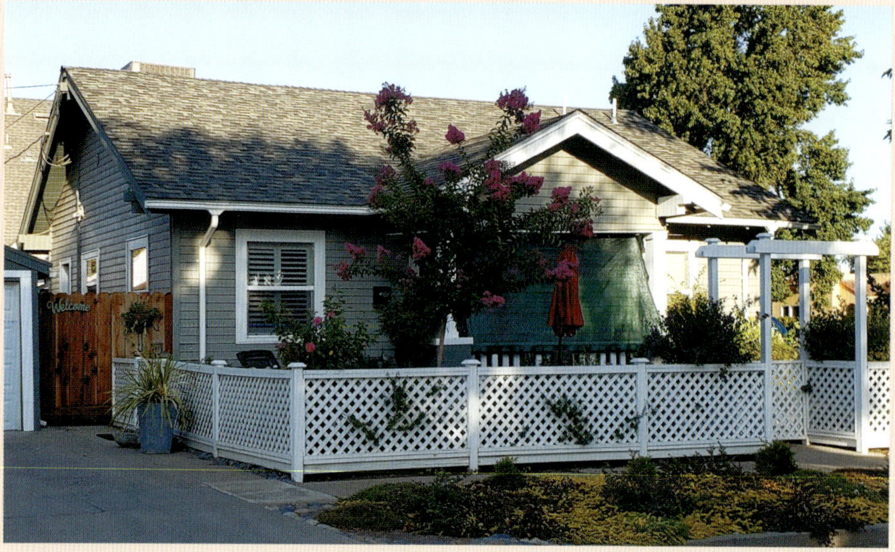

This very simple home was a residence of Leo and Wrotha Helton. In the 1950s, Leo owned a Chevron station at the corner of Highway 99 and Stockton Street. In 1958, he moved to Pine Street, opening a body shop and service station. Wrotha did not let the grass grow under her feet, either; she was an active member of the Woman's Christian Temperance Union and hosted meetings at this home. This group would make sure that the men of rest homes had magazines to read and supplied the ladies there with beautiful bouquets of flowers.

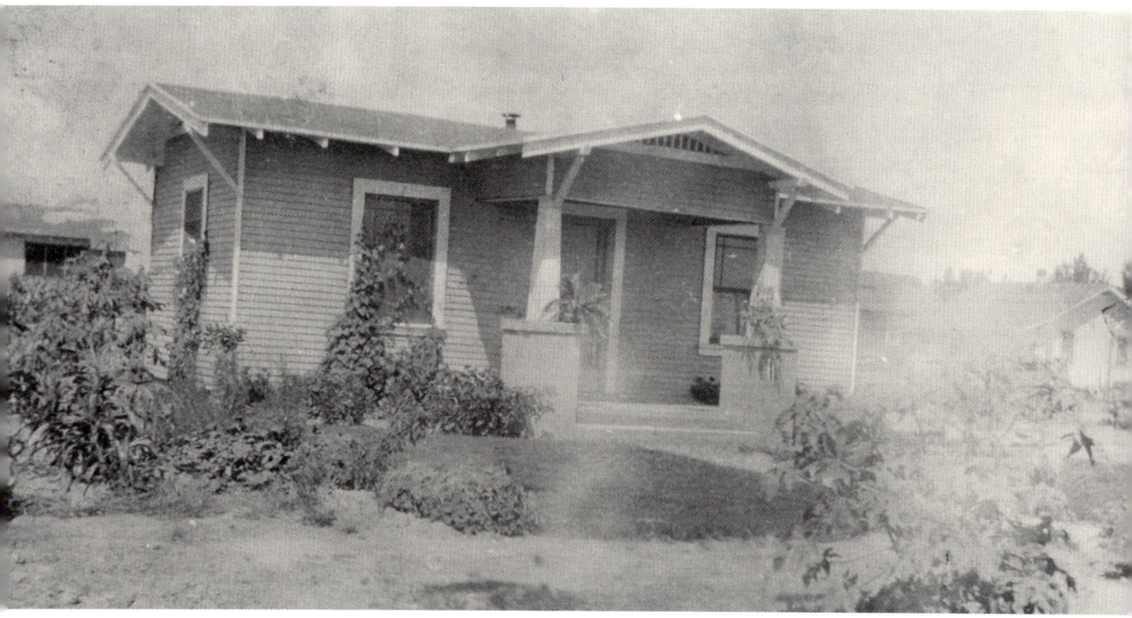

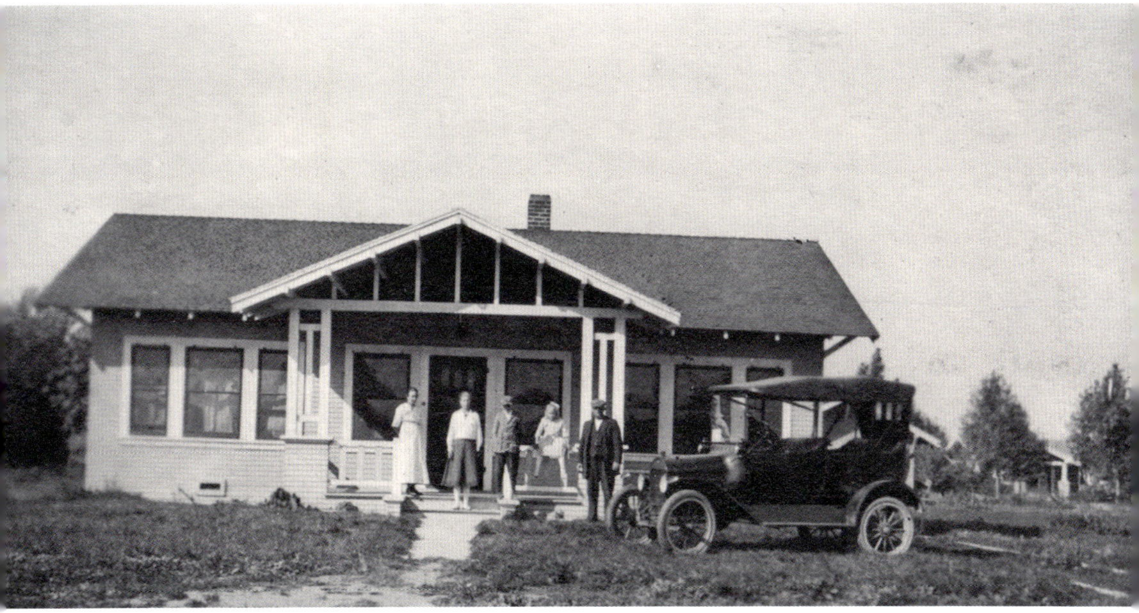

Edith Nelson was the occupant of this house from 1943 on, and she worked across the street at the Ripon Elementary School. She headed up the cafeteria until 1961, when she retired. Because of the house's close proximity to the church, church meetings were often held at Nelson's home. She was known as an incredible baker and always had cookies for the meetings. When school was out for the summer, Edith stayed busy working at Yosemite National Park and assisting at Camp Curry.

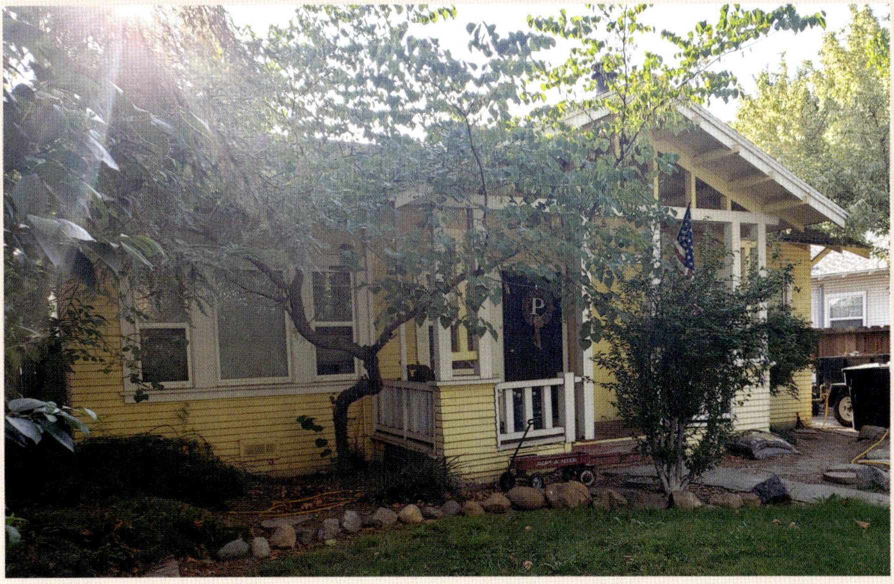

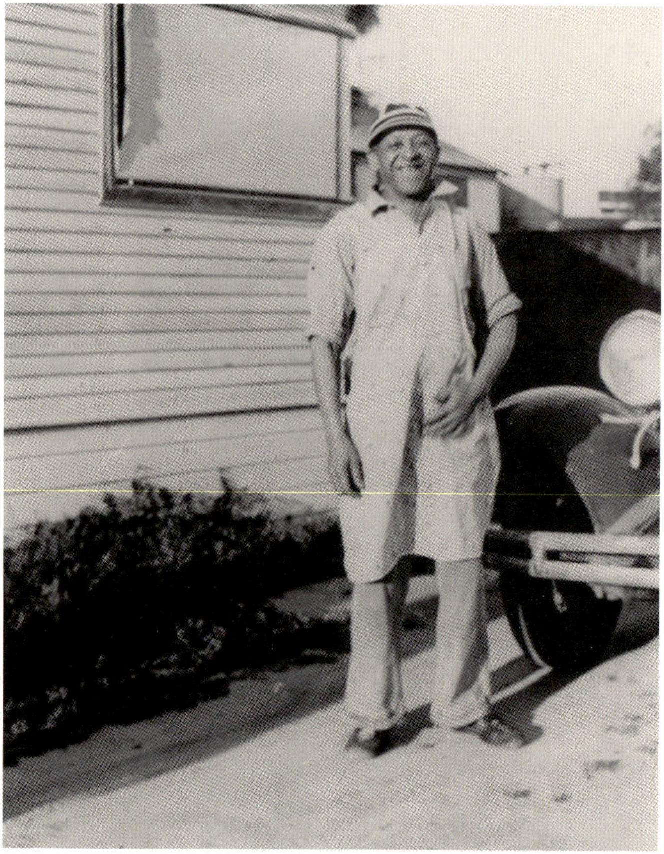

This was the home of Karl A. Gotshall, who held positions as vice president of the Bank of Ripon, manager of the Ripon Lumber Company, and secretary of the Central California Milk Producers Association and the Caswell Orphanage. Gotshall was very involved in the workings of Ripon. He passed away at a young age from the great plague on November 4, 1918, only nine years after his arrival to Ripon. After Karl's death, his widow, Helen Gotshall, remarried. This is a picture of Charlie Goodman, the family's cook and domestic helper.

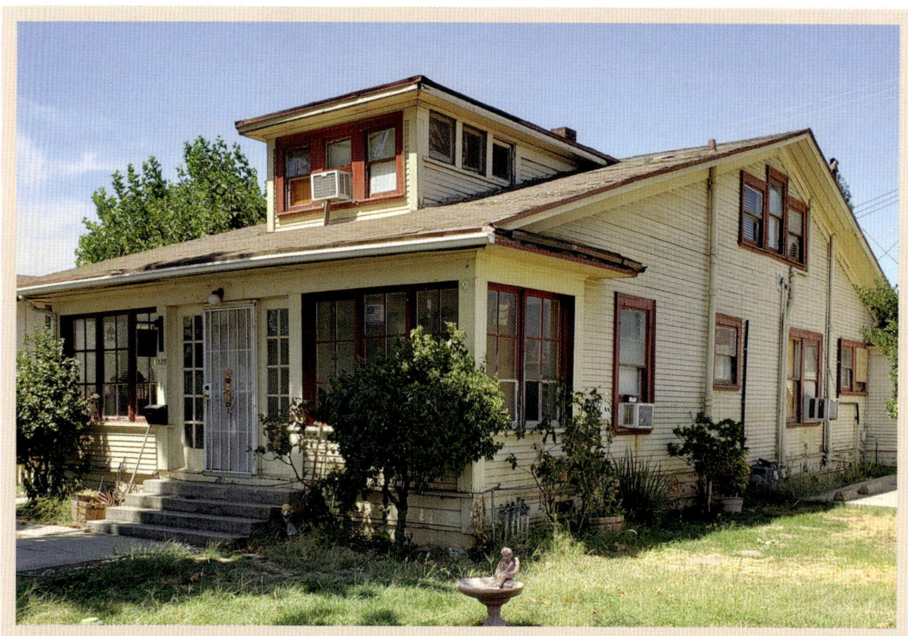

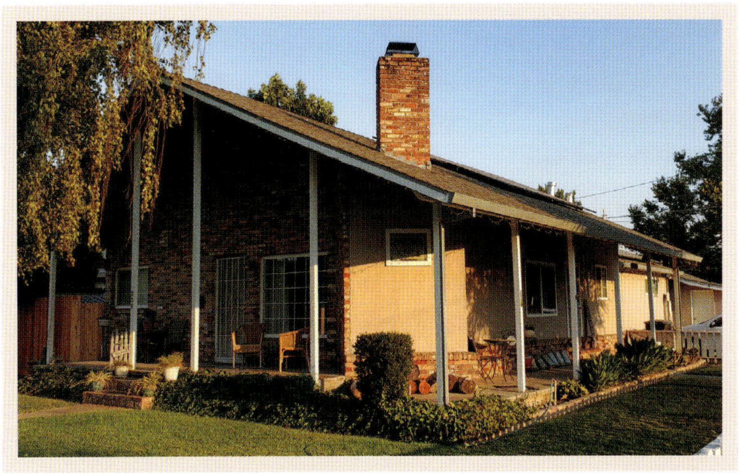

This was the home of George and Molly Markham, which sat on the corner of Main Street and what would become Stockton Street in 1905. In the background of the photograph, the headstones of the Ripon Cemetery are visible across the county road. In 1921, the home was moved to make room for the construction of a new bank. The house shown in the now picture is the extensively remodeled Markham home on First Street.

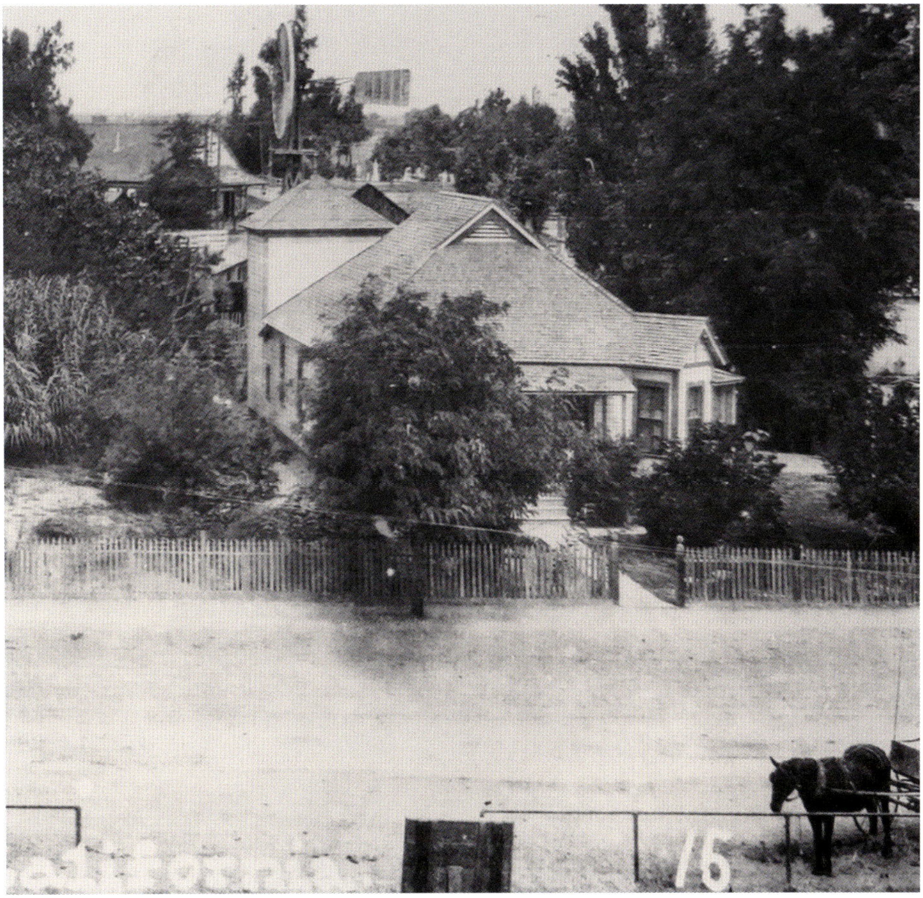

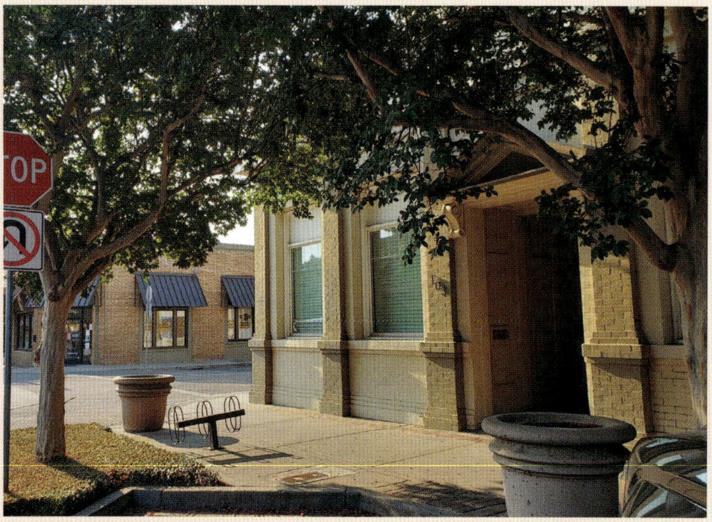

This photograph was taken in 1913 as these gentlemen were getting their cars ready to go on a rally to the dedication of the Goodwin Down. These gentlemen were the "who's who" of Ripon society: Syd Reynolds, Frank Mckee, Irving Goodwin, Charles Frederick, Tom Smethers, Lynn Garner, and Jim Speaker—all businessmen or bankers. In the background are the Bank of Ripon and the Markham home (before it was moved to First Street to make room for the new bank in 1921). (Past image courtesy of Ripon Historical Society.)

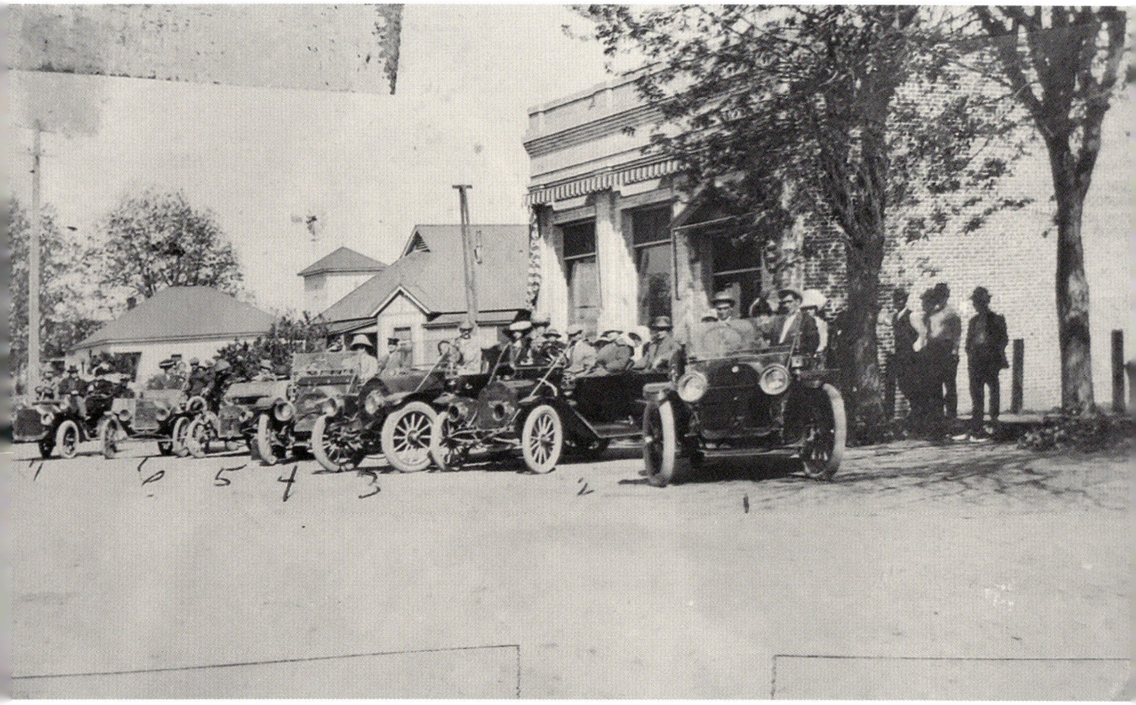

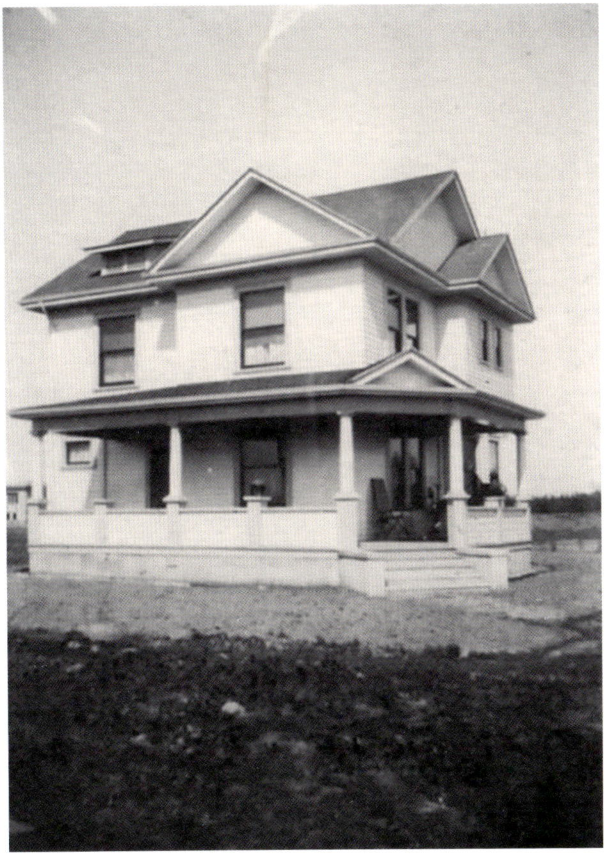

This is the Nancy Curtis home, which was built in 1912. In 1882, Melvin Curtis, age 24, married Nancy Fredericks, age 17. Melvin amassed a fortune from being a stockholder in the Electric Railroad, which was being built from Stockton to Modesto, and the Ripon Meat Company. Sadly, in 1909, he committed suicide. At the time of his death, he was one of the wealthiest farmers in the region. In the 1960s, the house was remodeled; the beautiful columns that were on the outside porch are still visible.

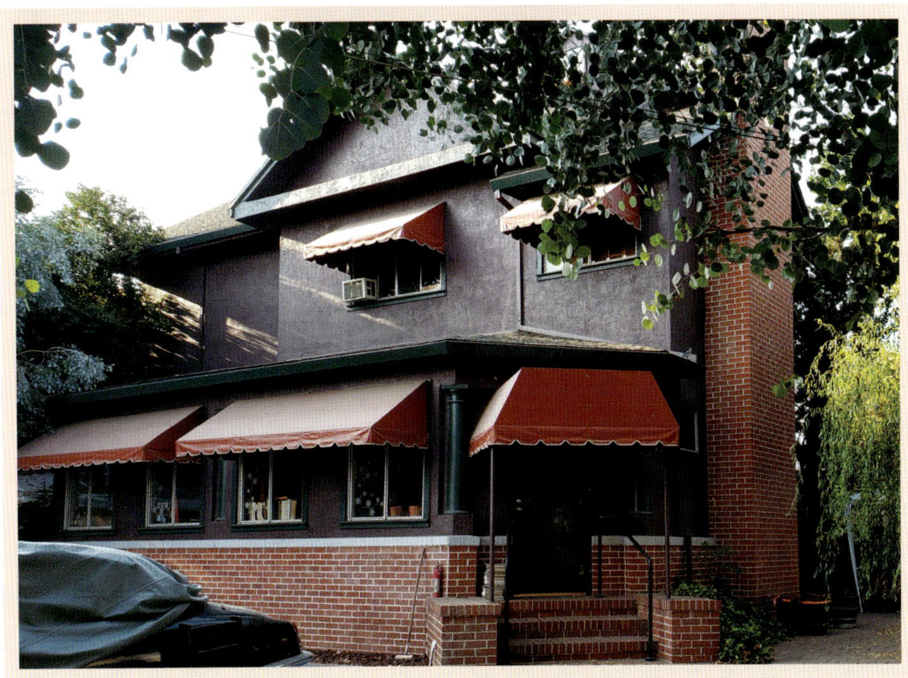

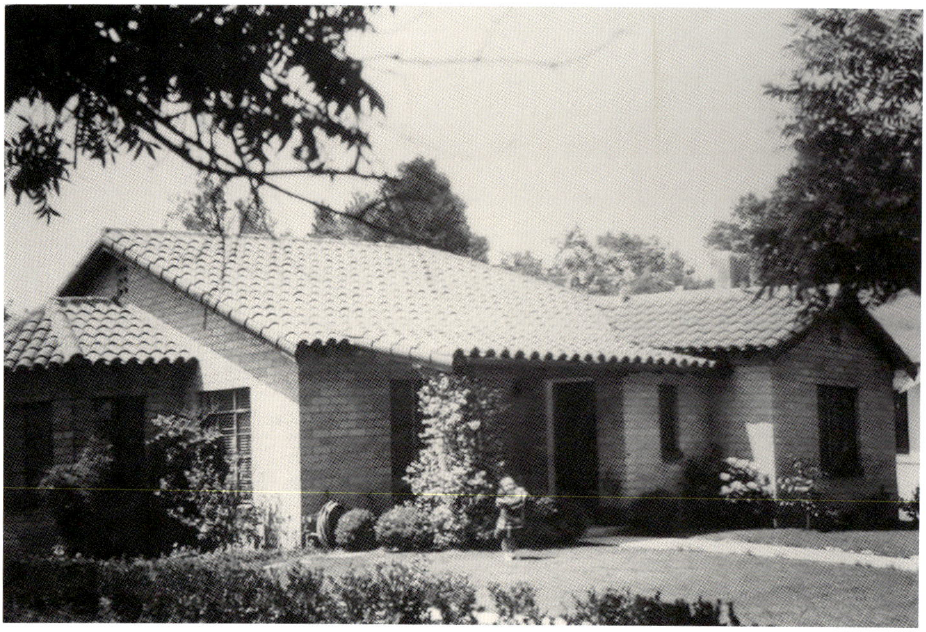

In 1948, John Kamps built this lovely home at 412 First Street for the Bert J. Huber family. Huber was the assistant postmaster for 37 years, making sure that Ripon residents got their mail. Huber also served as a Ripon city councilman and mayor. Kamps, along with Jake Meeuwse, the brickmason and a relative of Huber, must have liked the design, because just two blocks down, he used the exact same design for a home at 634 W. Main Street for another family. (Past image courtesy of the Huber family.)

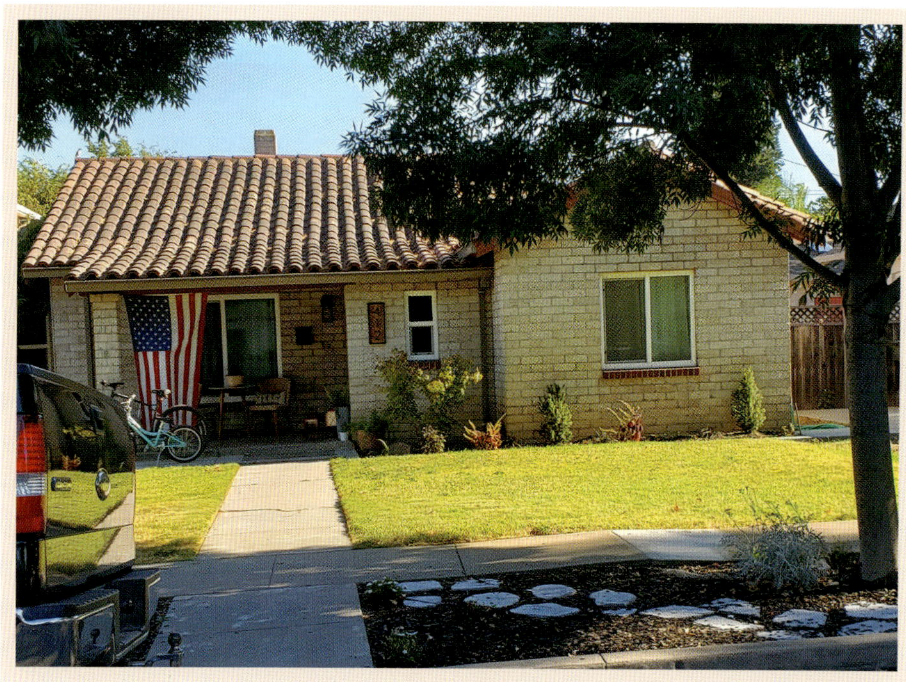

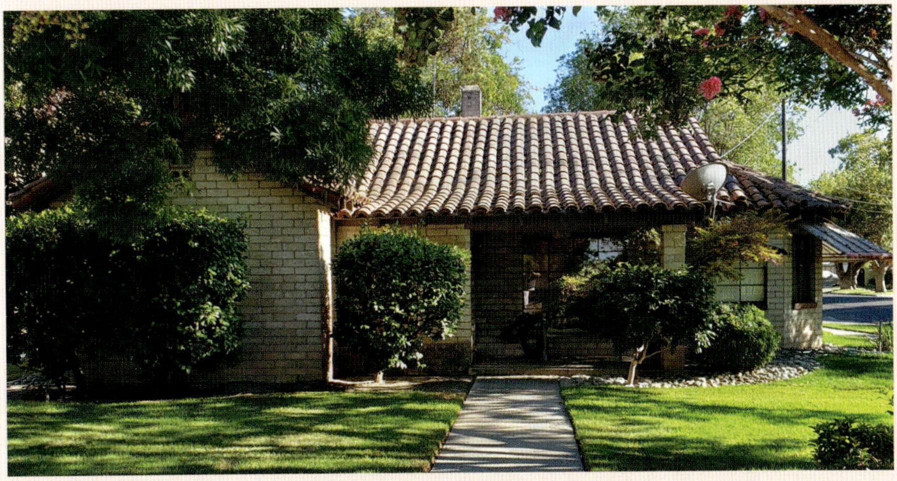

This home was a replica of the house that John Kamps built at 412 First Street; both of the homes appear to be Spanish Mission Revival style. The roofline is the same, with both having gable roofs covered with terra-cotta tile. The same metal multipaned windows were used on both homes. Kamps, along with brickmason Jake Meeuwse, actually created three homes in this same style. It appears that Kamps used the same blueprints in the designs of all three homes. (Past image courtesy of the Huber family.)

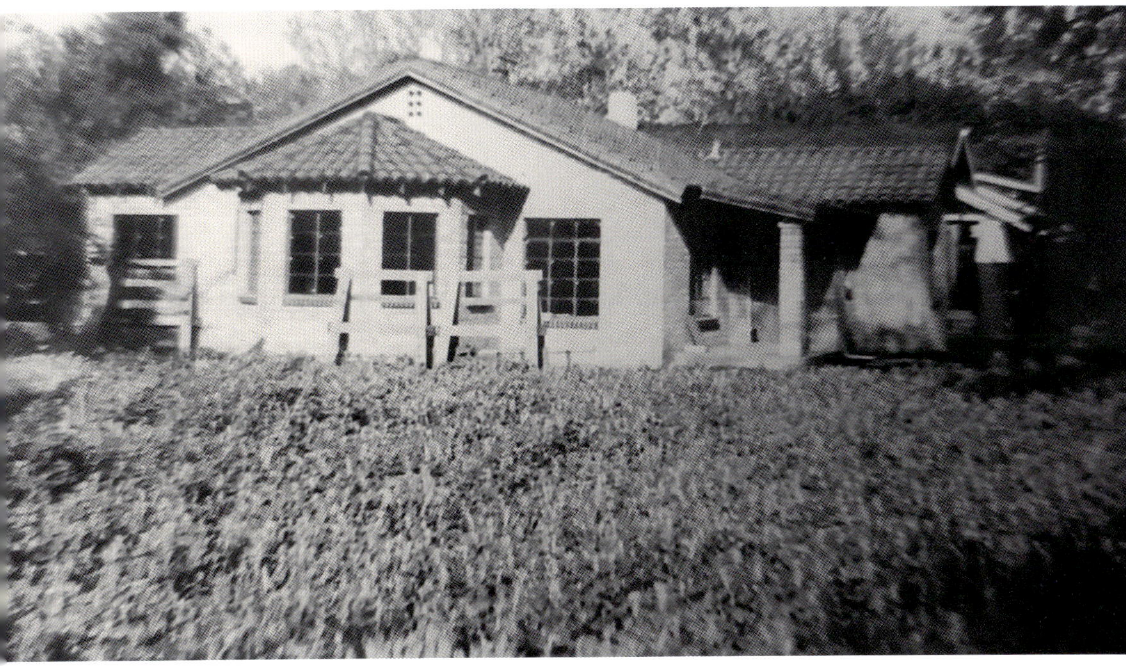

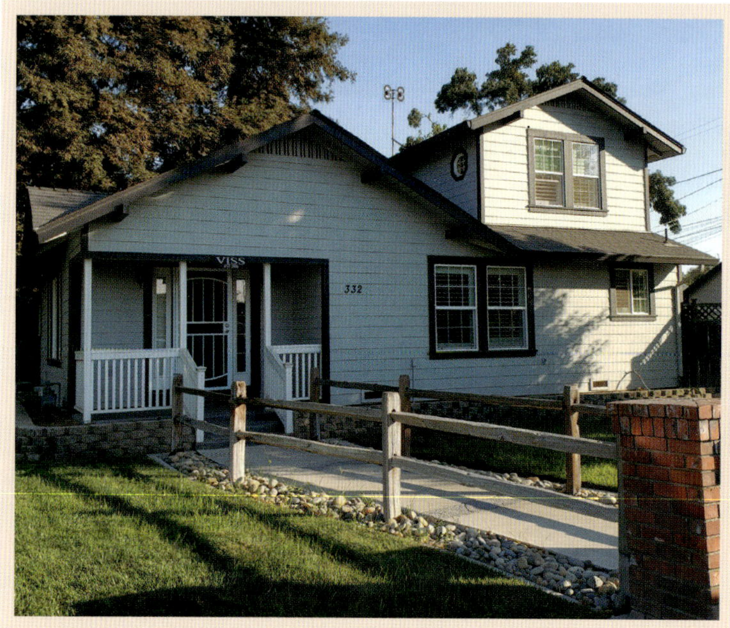

This farmhouse was built in 1935 by John Nykant, who was in the construction business and had a hand in erecting many homes in Ripon. The home originally sat on W. Ripon Road; 60 years later, the home was in a new place on Quiet Street on the other side of town. Development was coming through, and Bethany Home Society wished to build apartments. The structure was offered to Nicholas Viss for $1, and he bought it. Being a carpenter, Viss did a fine job on the home. (Past image courtesy of the Huber family.)

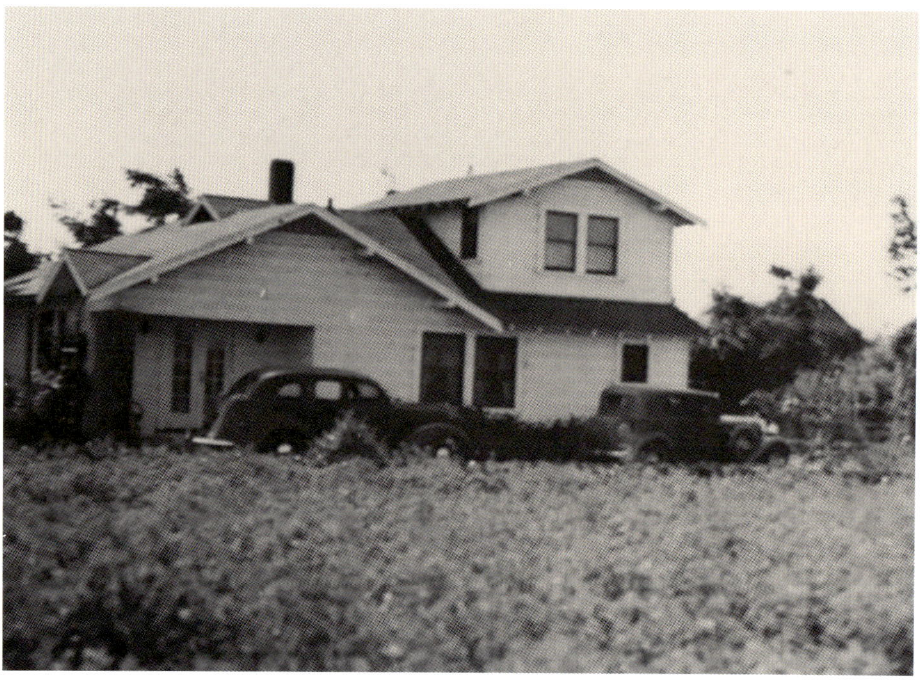

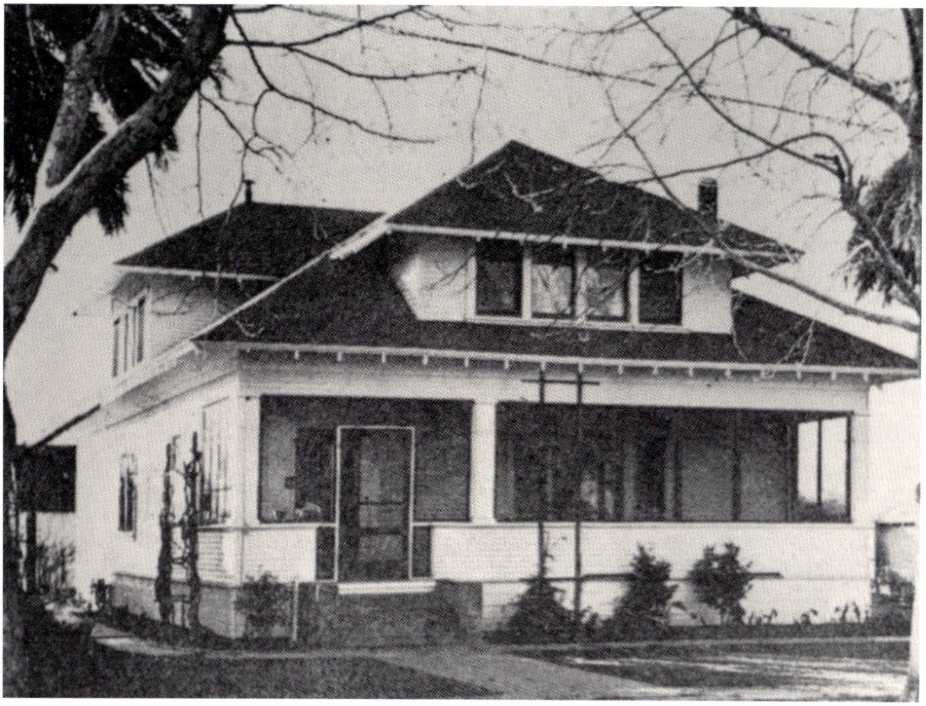

This beautiful home was built in 1912 by A.J. Nourse. In 1919, the home was purchased by the First Christian Reform Church for use as a parsonage. In August 1926, the home had a little bit of excitement it did not need. The Ripon Hospital burned to the ground, and a number of patients were brought to the parsonage, which was used as a temporary hospital. In 1976, it was moved to a new location at 809 Palm Avenue, and the church built a new parsonage.

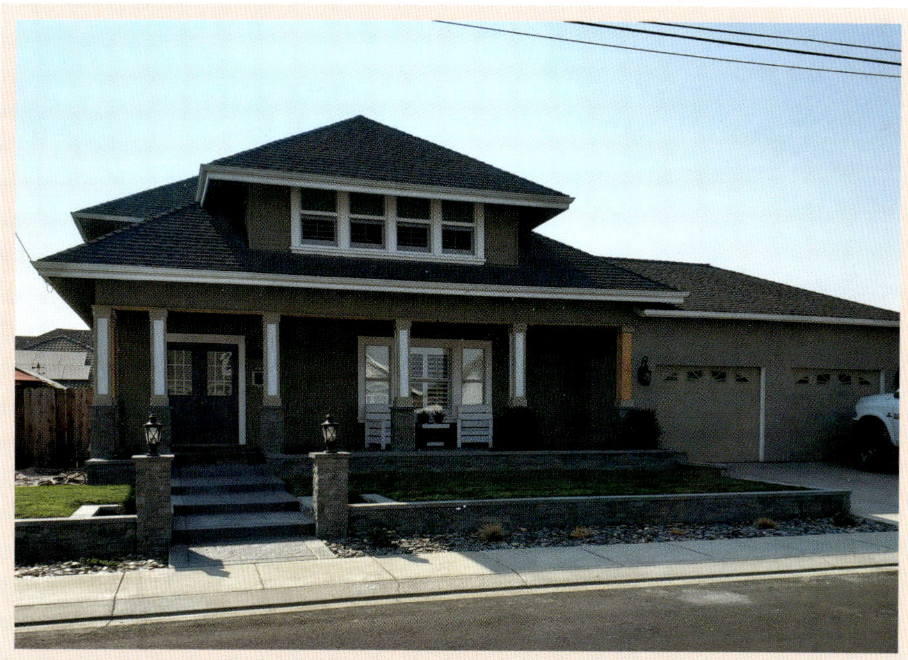

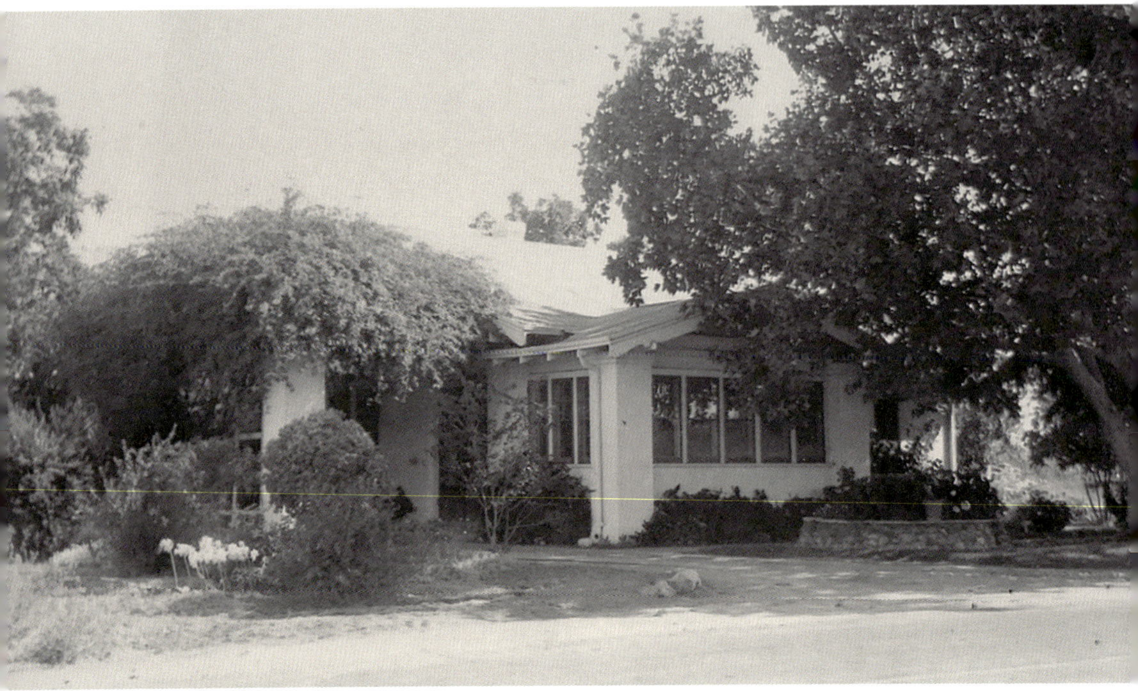

This home was built in 1923, but the garage of the home was constructed first so the homeowner could live in the garage while waiting for the home to be finished. In 1947, Mike and Elsie Stewart purchased the beautiful home for $13,500, although Mike's father felt that was a bit too much money. Obviously, it was a good investment, as Mike's son Jim and his wife, Kathy, now live in the home, and the third generation of Stewarts gather there for family dinners, with the fourth-generation grandkids playing in the yard. (Past image courtesy of the Stewart family.)

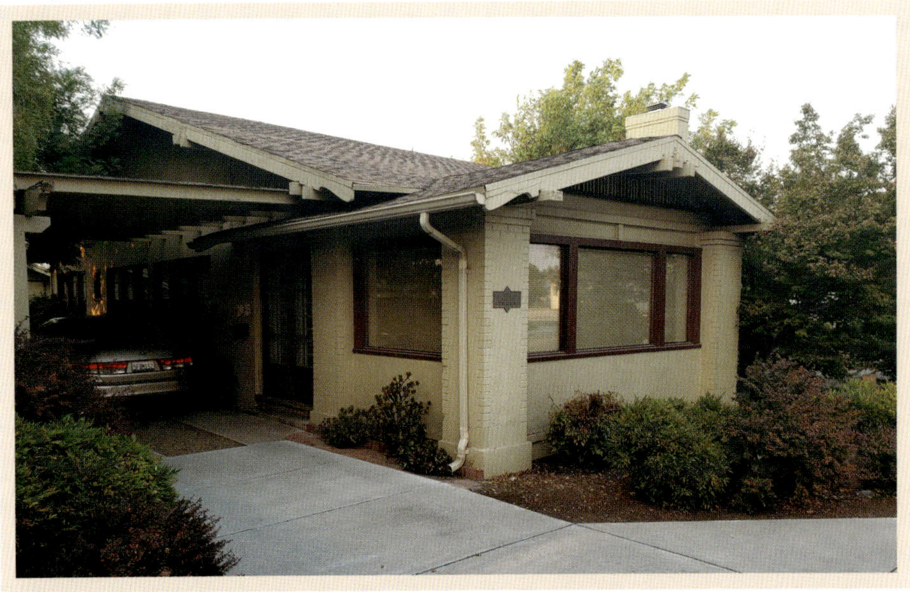

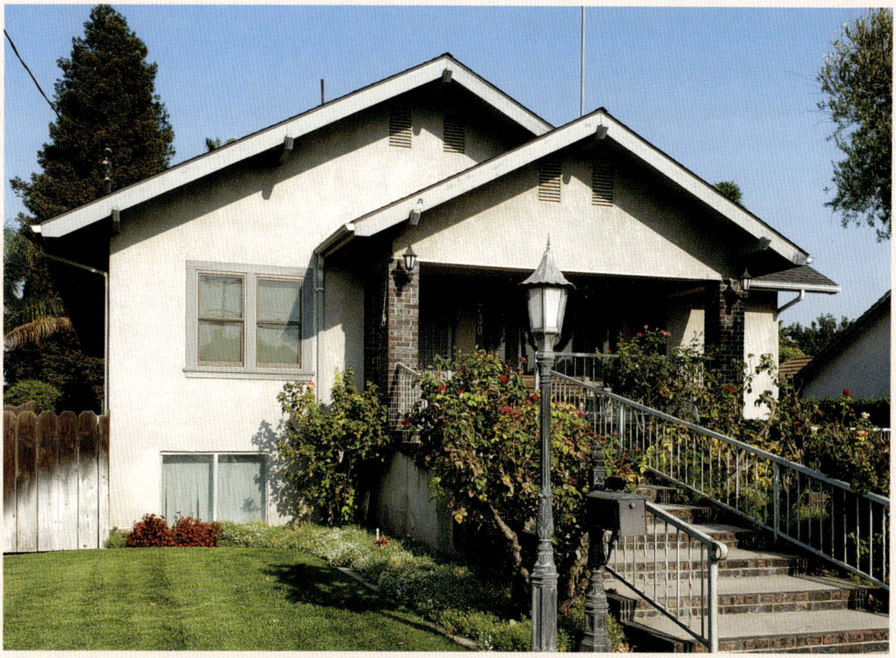

This farmhouse was built in 1917. It was the home of Gerald and Adriana Miedema for many years. In 1995, Ripon was getting a highly anticipated McDonald's, and the home needed to be moved. Landowners Randy and Dawn Eskes decided that they wanted the house. In the vintage picture, it is in the process of being moved from the corner of Main Street and Wilma Avenue. The Eskes added a basement, which made the house much taller. It is shown in the current image at 730 Palm Avenue. (Past image courtesy of the Eskes family.)

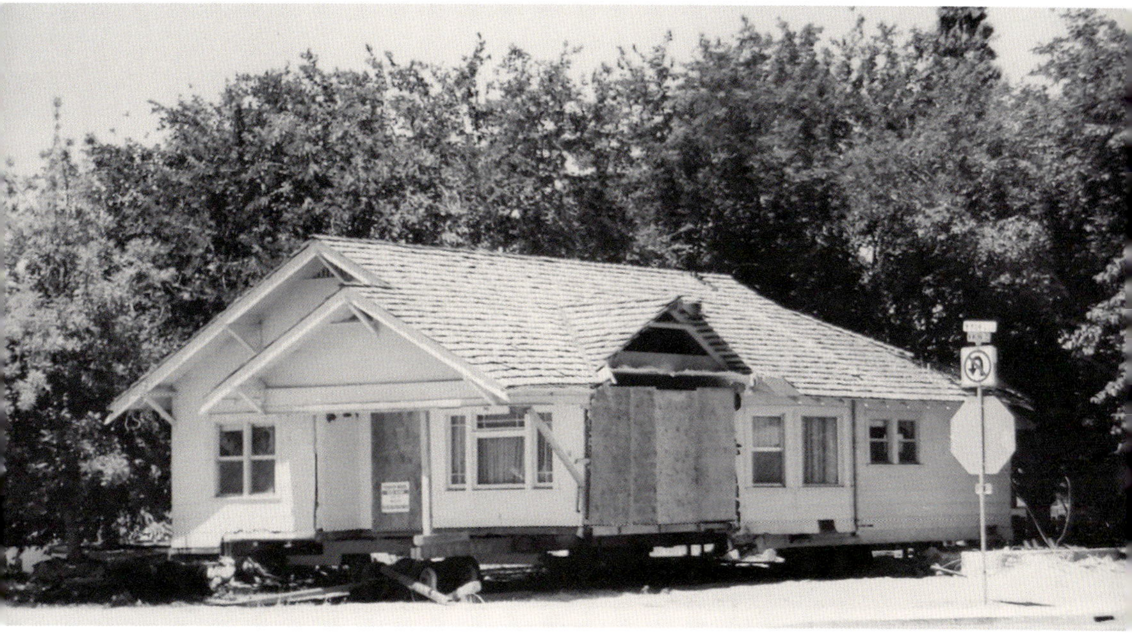

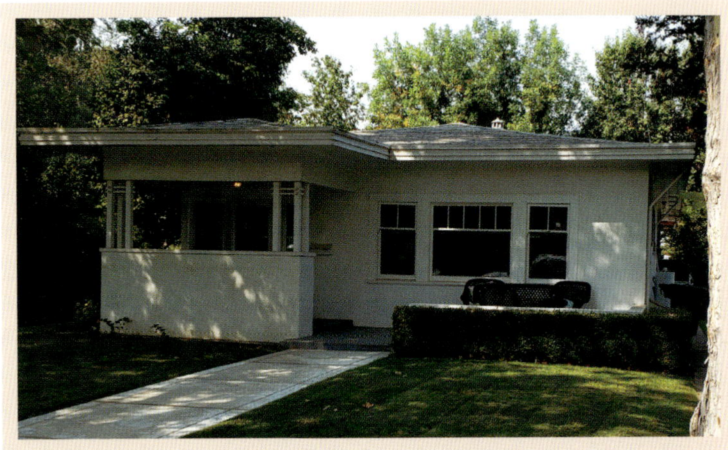

Alney J. "A.J." Nourse began his career in Ripon in 1897 when he took over management of the 800-acre Cady Ranch. In 1900, he purchased the ranch, adding 300 additional acres. In 1919, Nourse sold his stately home to a church for use as a parsonage. The newspaper proclaimed Nourse was building a beautiful bungalow on Orange Avenue. By 1928, Nourse had owned the Ripon Water Company and Nourse Hardware Company and was a stockholder in Ripon Lumber Company and vice president of the Bank of Ripon—he was a busy man.

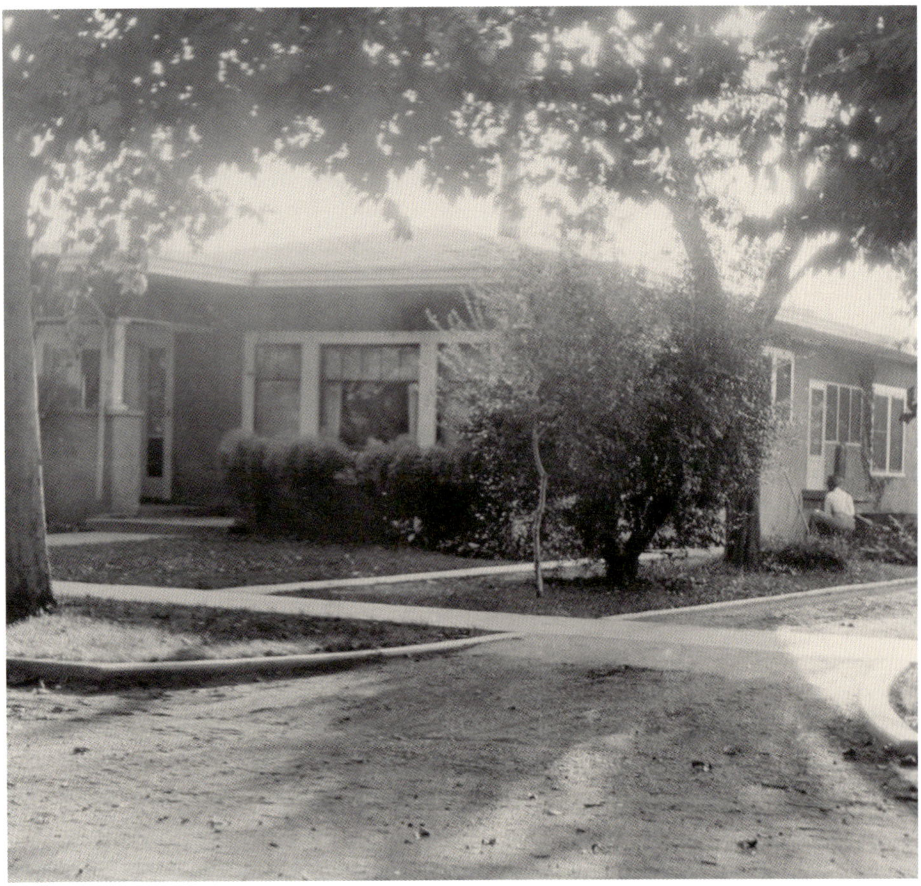

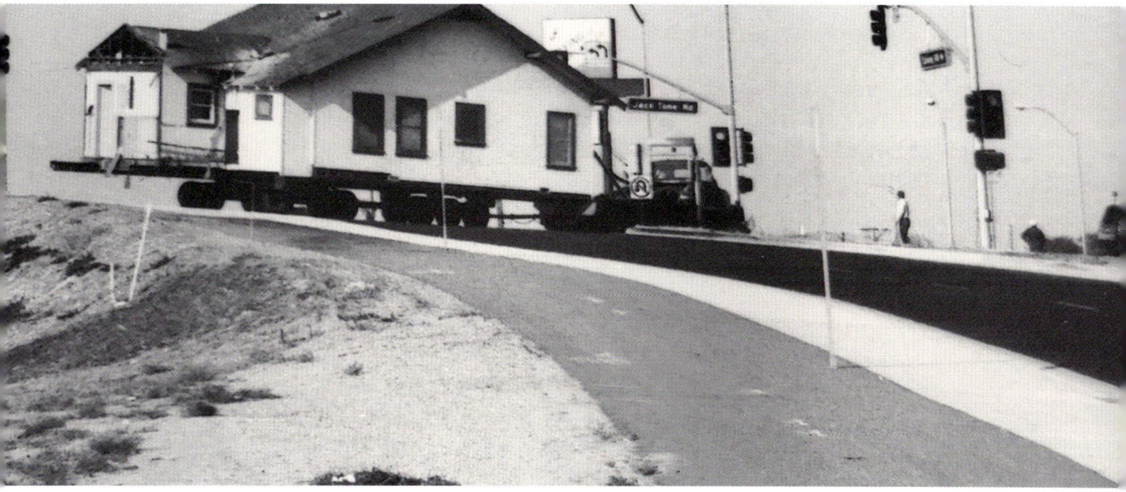

This home was originally built in 1926 at 702 Jack Tone Road. In 2002, Jim and Viv Schuller discovered that the house was slated for demolition, so they asked Bill Kamps if they could buy it and have it moved to a location on S. Olive Avenue. Kamps said yes, and Jim handed him a silver dollar. The silver dollar was cheap, but the $5,000 moving of the house was not. Now, it sits on five beautiful acres, much like it did when it was a farmhouse in 1926. (Past image courtesy of the Schuller family.)

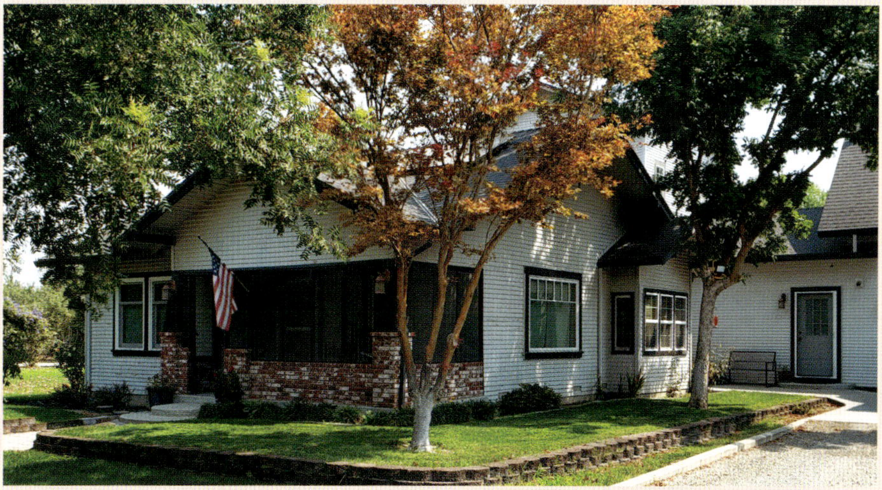

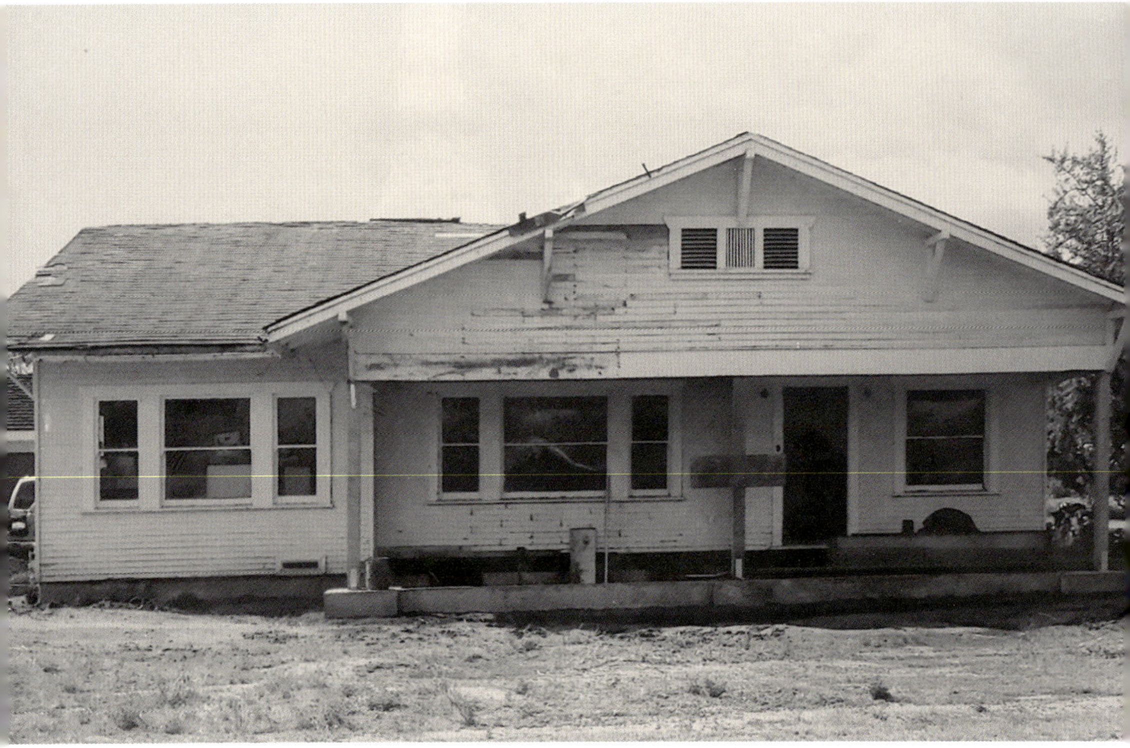

This house was built in 1905. In 1947, the Vander Laans bought the home and raised a family there. It was home to many families after that, but the most significant change came in 1999. After a two-year stay in Europe, the Enserinks rented the home. Steve and Shirley Enserink had grown to appreciate the quality and uniqueness of the Arts and Crafts–style bungalow, but the church needed more room, and the home was slated for demolition. Instead of the home being destroyed, Steve Enserink purchased, moved, and preserved it. (Past image courtesy of the Enserink family.)

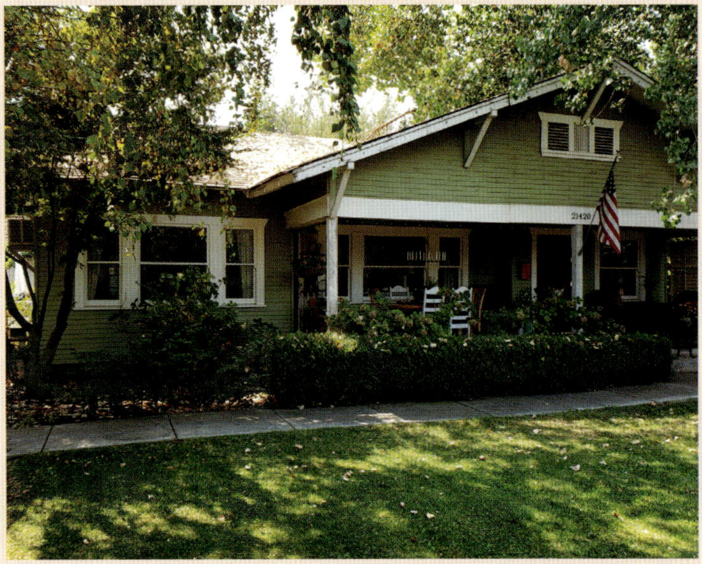

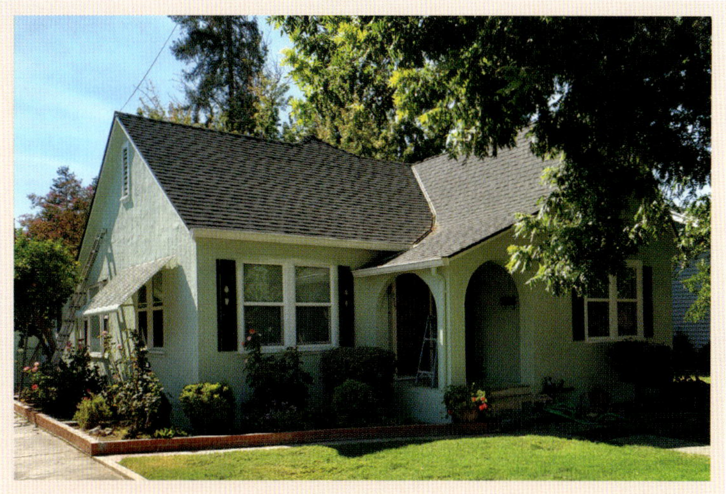

The Burnell family moved to Ripon in 1937 and made their home in this lovely cottage. They owned the Burnell market at the corner of Stockton and Main Streets. In 1954, Genevieve Burnell had heart surgery at Stanford Hospital. The surgery made the papers, as it was cutting-edge at the time —it was called "knife finger surgery" because a knife was attached to the finger of the surgeon. In 1987, Pat Meendering, a Ripon Christian third-grade teacher, moved into the home and has lovingly cared for it since then.

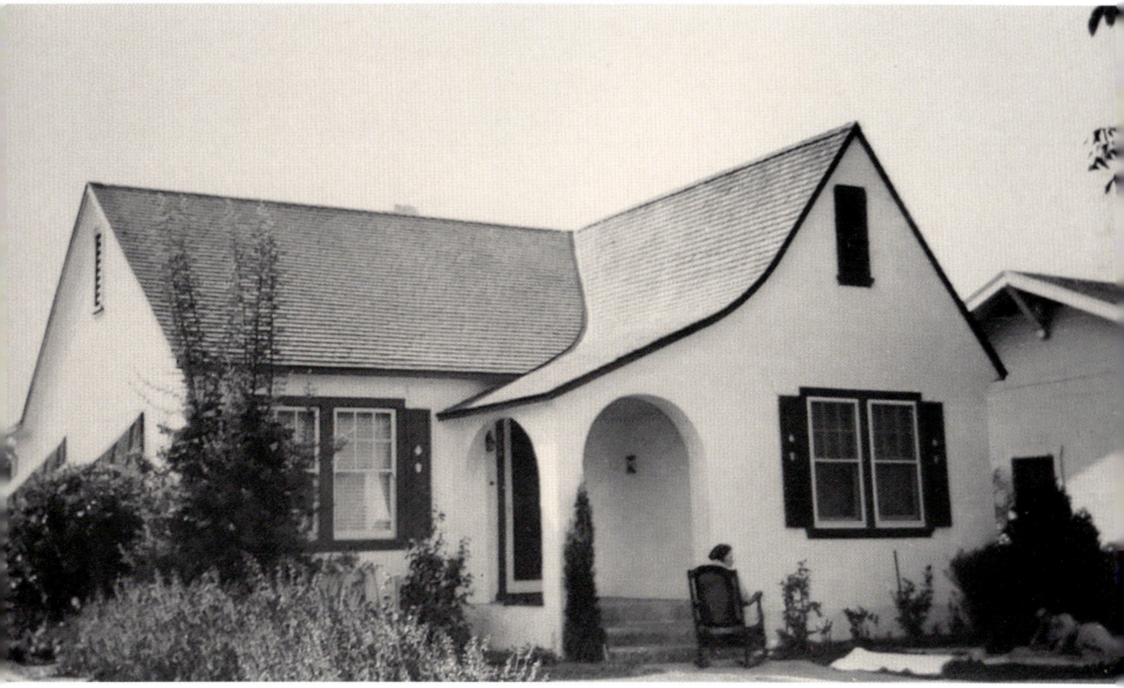

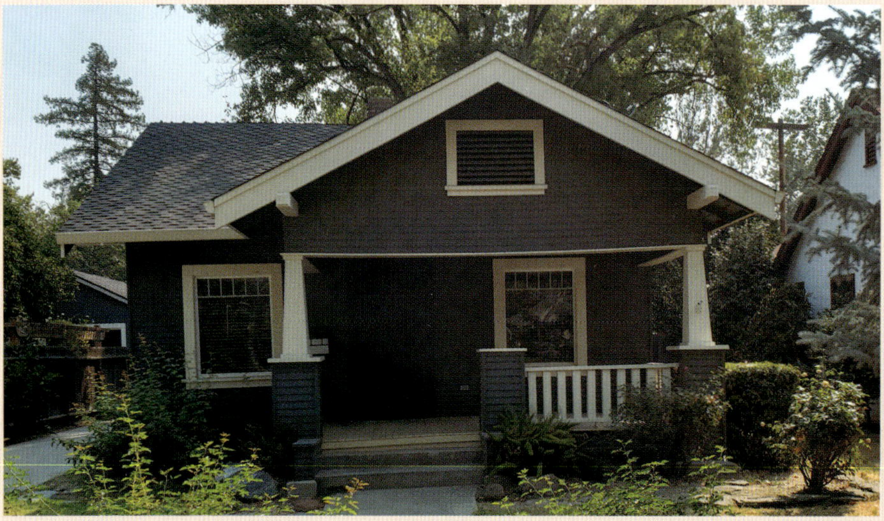

This lovely image of a young girl in the field was captured in 1916. On the far right in the photograph is the home that Genova Fredericks had built for use as a rental. Because of the extensive wealth of the Fredericks family, none of the daughters ever worked, but Genova Fredericks always lived by a saying: "It is nice to be important, but it is more important to be nice." She gave extensively to the community and cared deeply for the people of Ripon.

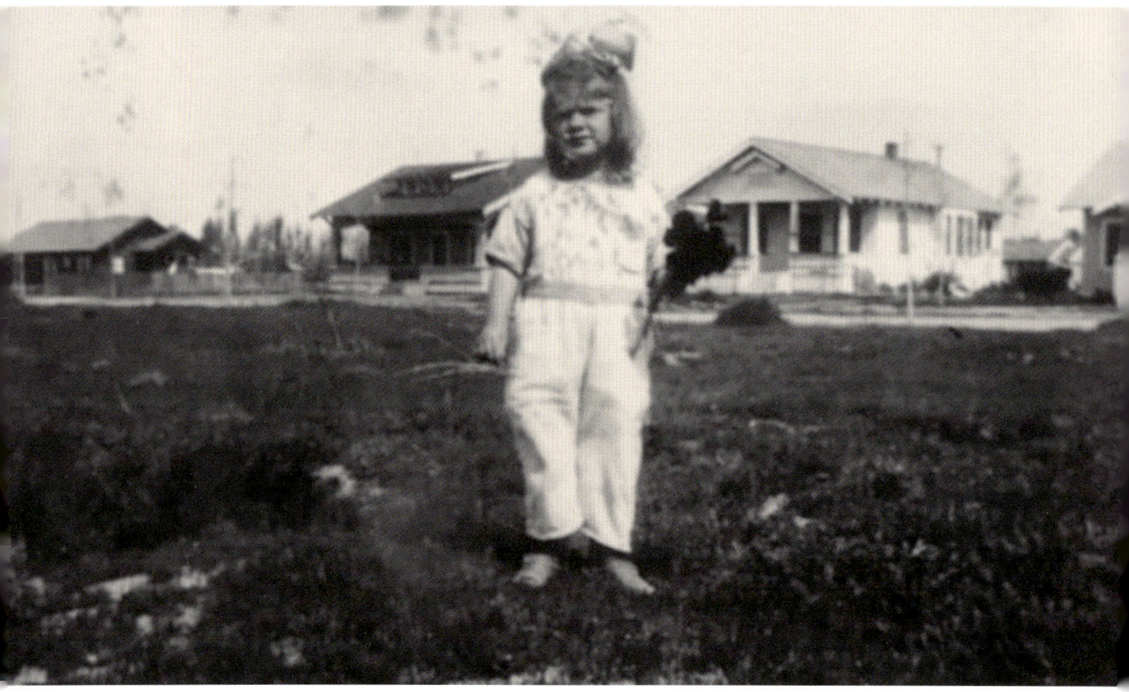

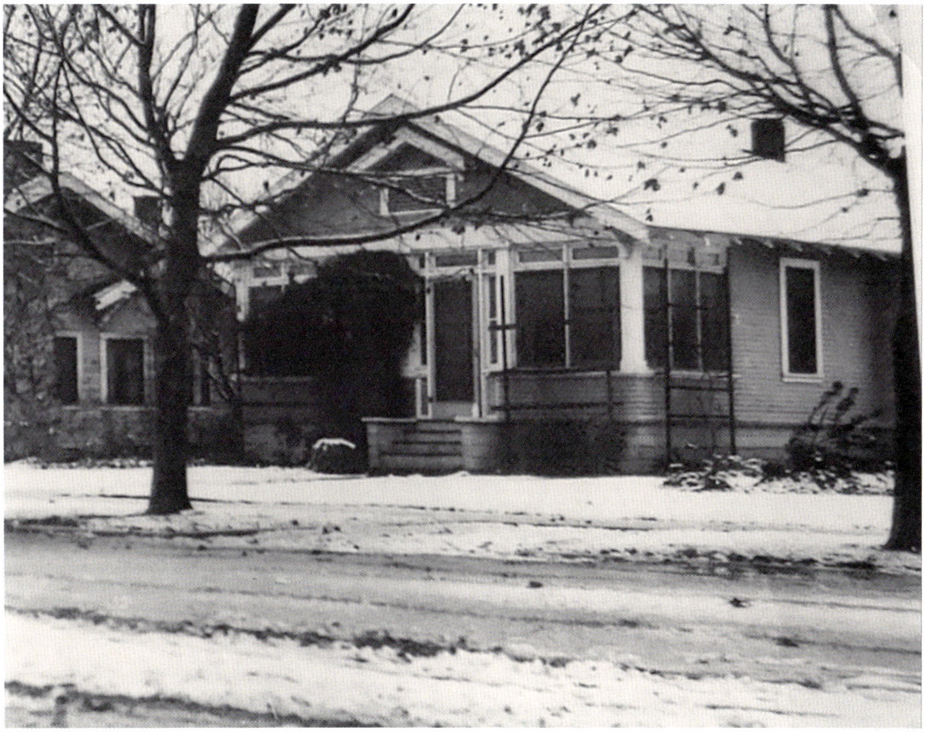

Genova Fredericks's home is pictured on a snowy day in 1922. The home was built in 1913 (followed by two adjacent homes built in 1913 and 1921) for the Fredericks sisters and their families. Genova Fredericks was at the center of social activities of Ripon. In 1924, the Women's Improvement Club was looking for a building for a community hall and chamber of commerce office. Genova stepped up, paying for the group to buy First Christian Reformed Church and two empty lots—this is just one example of how she contributed to the betterment of her community. (Past image courtesy of LuAnn Vander Meulen.)

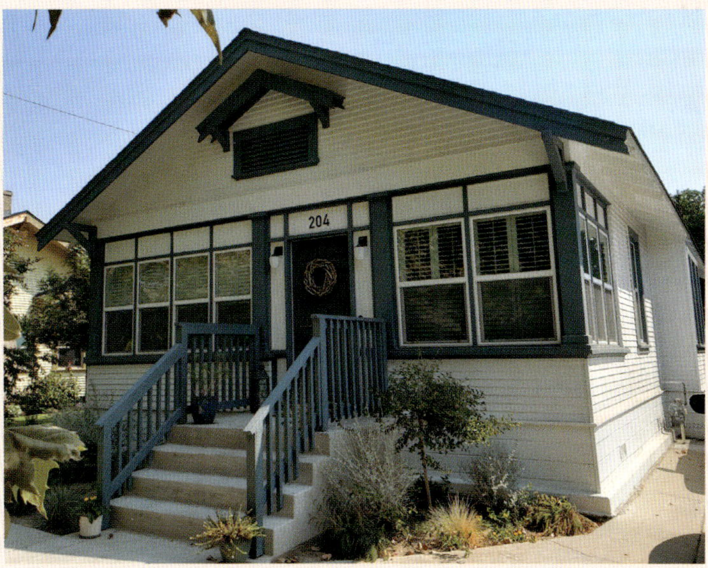

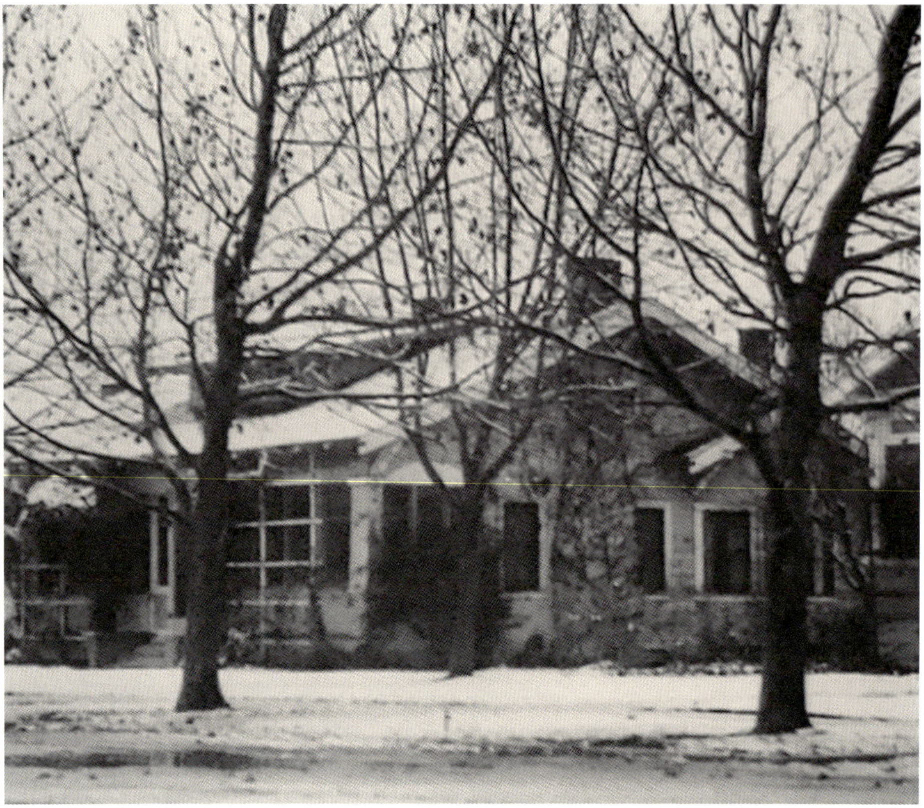

Hugh Leavitt and Lulu (Fredericks) Dickey were major players in the Ripon social scene. Lulu was from the pioneer Thomas Fredericks family, and Hugh became president of the Bank of Ripon in 1912. Although the bank was sold to Bank of America in 1920, Hugh remained president until his retirement in 1935. Lulu was very fortunate, as the houses on either side of her were occupied by Hattie and Genova Fredericks. Now a third generation lives in the home—Robert and LuAnn Vander Meulen (LuAnn is the granddaughter of Hugh Leavitt). (Past image courtesy of LuAnn Vander Meulen.)

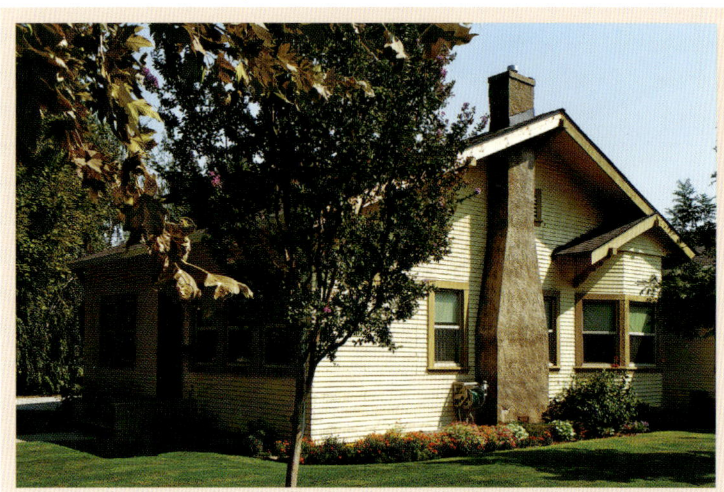

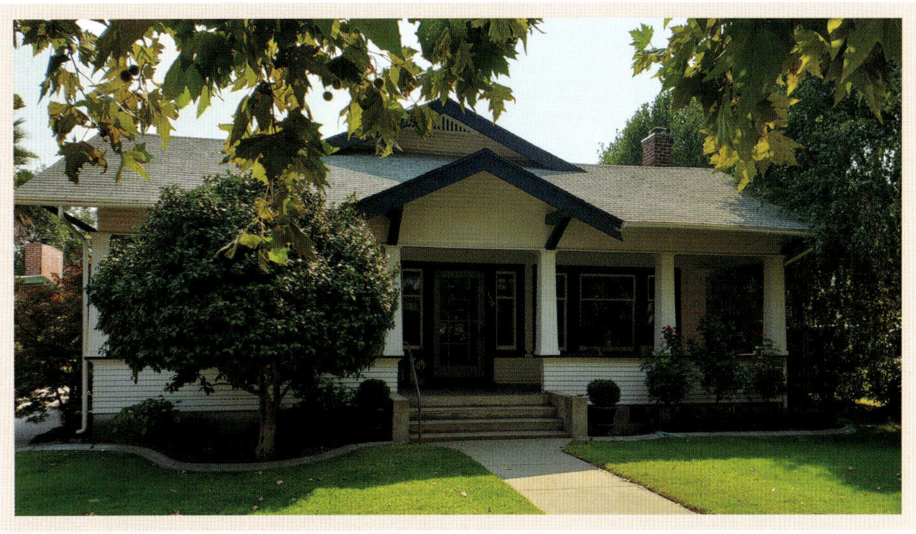

After the death of Thomas Fredericks in 1920, his wife, Susan (Crow) Fredericks, sold her home in Stockton and moved back to Ripon to be near her daughters. This stately home, built in 1921 by contractor C.C. Bosch, is pictured on a snowy day in 1922. Hattie Fredericks, Susan's daughter, lived with her mother until Susan's death. Hattie inherited the home and continued to live her active social life. Hattie was born in 1877, and she lived in this house until her death in 1975. (Past image courtesy of LuAnn Vander Meulen.)

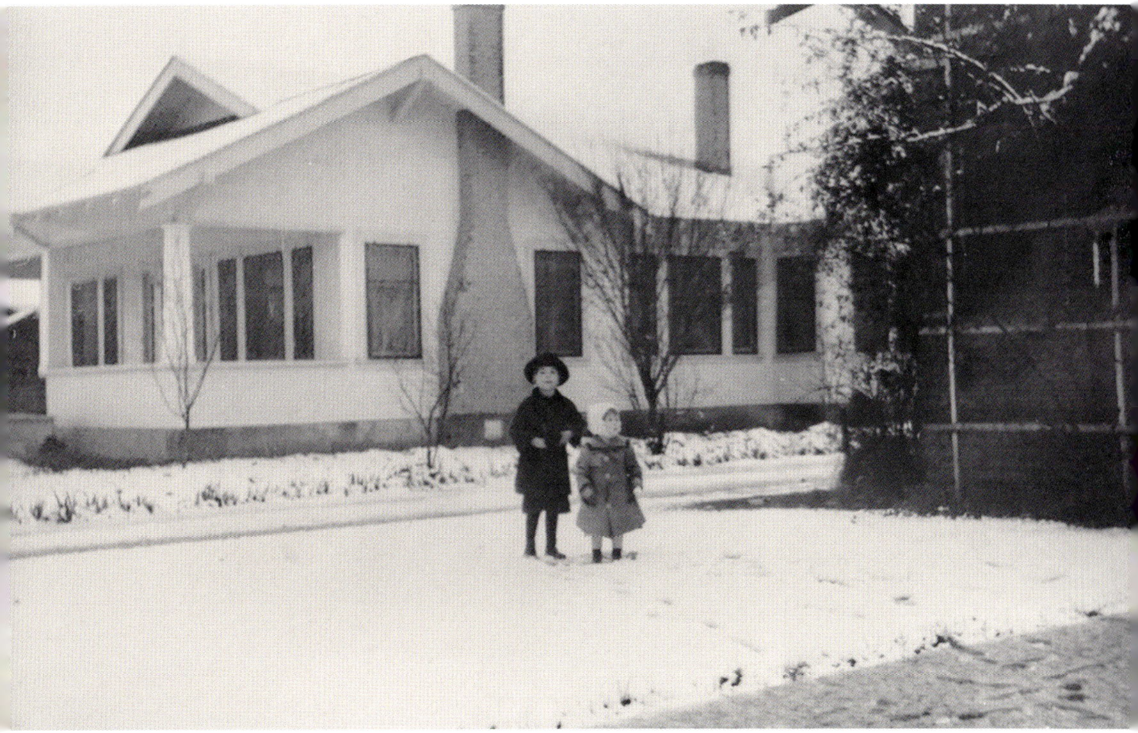

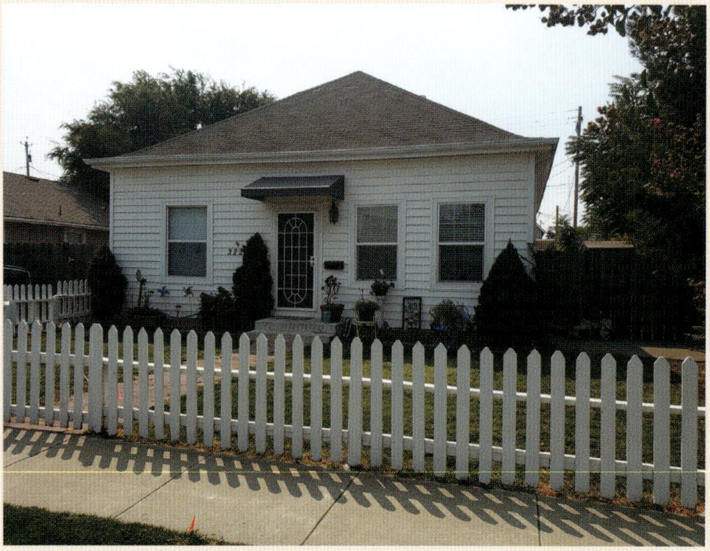

This home was on Main Street near where Walnut Avenue is now. It was the home of Sidney W. Reynolds and his wife, Mable. In 1910, Mable died after childbirth. Sidney remarried in 1913 and built a new home on Orange Avenue, and his old house was moved to First Street. In 1918, he got into the olive business, planting a 60-acre grove on the outskirts of Ripon; this grove was the first of its kind in the area. The location of the grove is now home to Spring Creek Country Club.

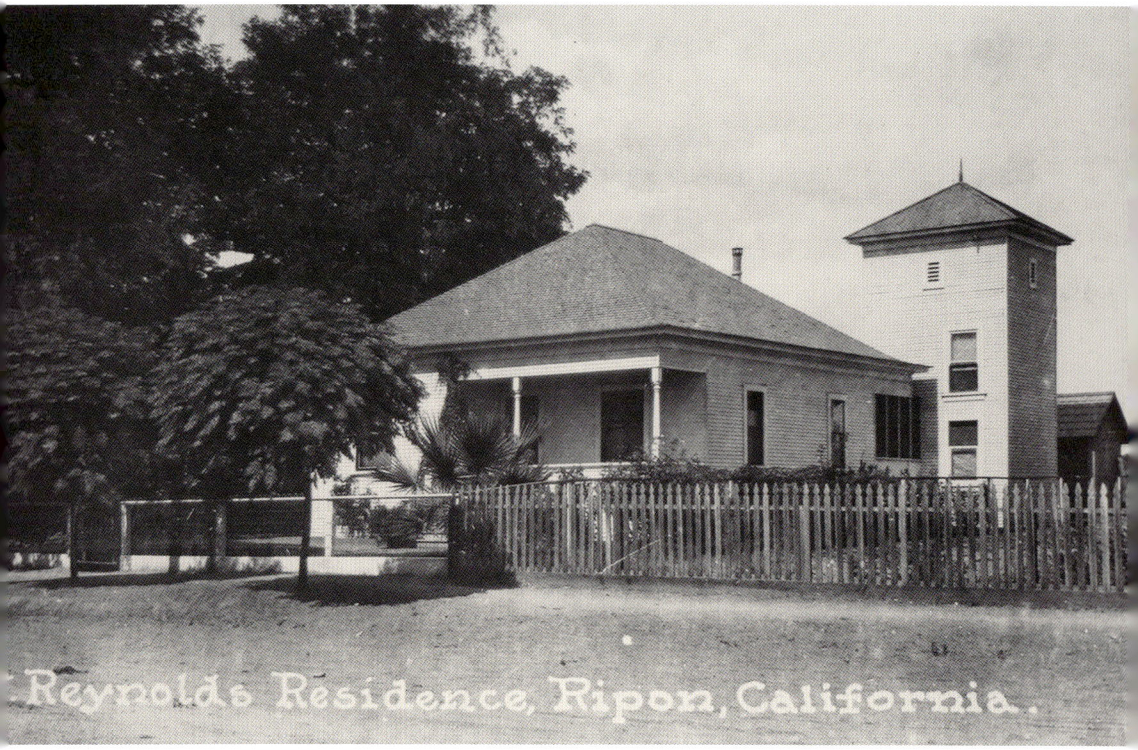

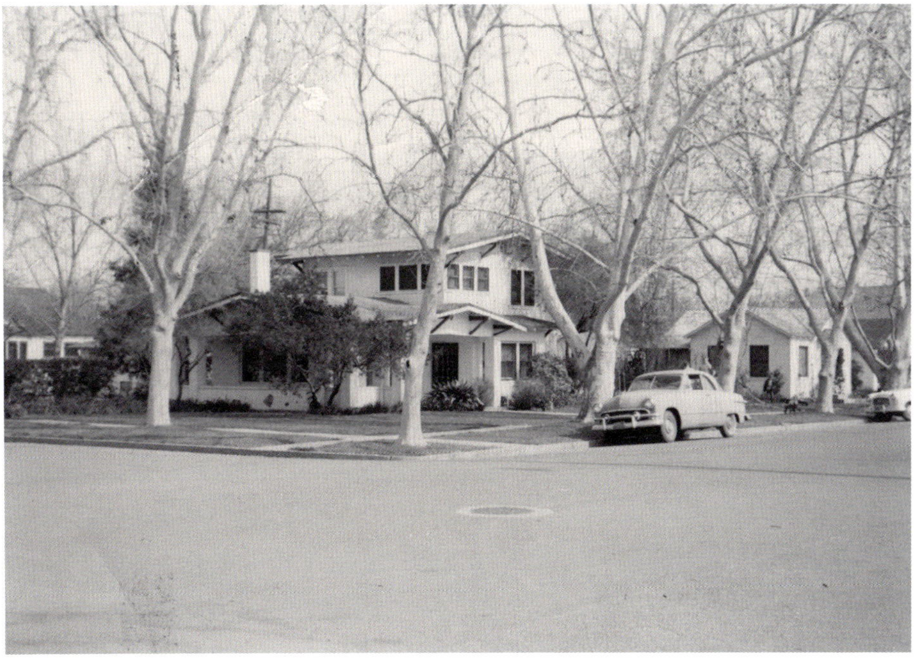

In 1935, the Calvary Reformed Church was growing and needed a pastor to guide the congregation. Rev. Edward Fikse arrived with his family, so a parsonage was needed. This beautiful home was purchased for the pastor and his family. As the church grew, new pastors arrived to guide the flock, and a brand-new parsonage was built. As the church expanded, more room was needed, so the home was moved one and a half miles outside of town to start its new life.

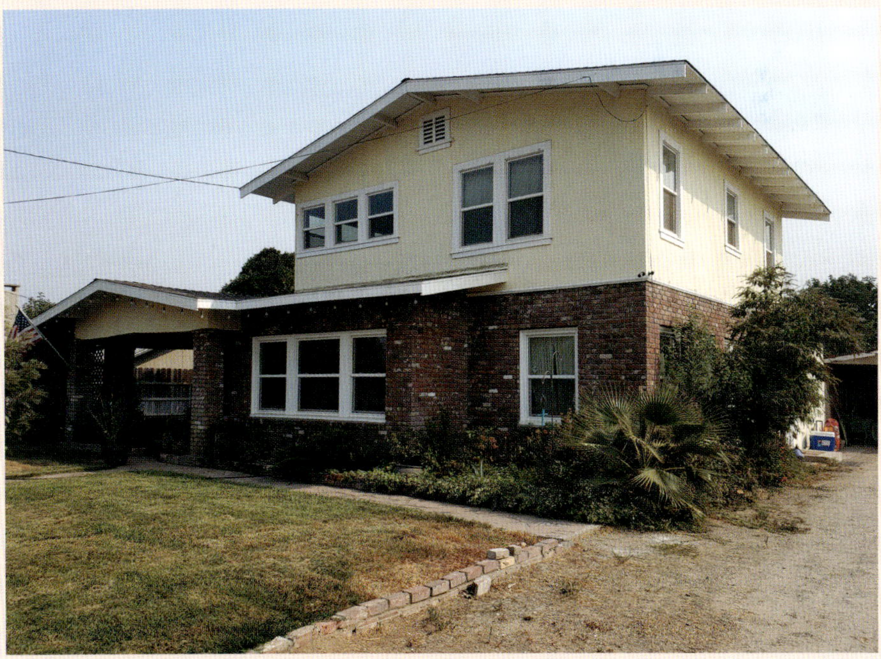

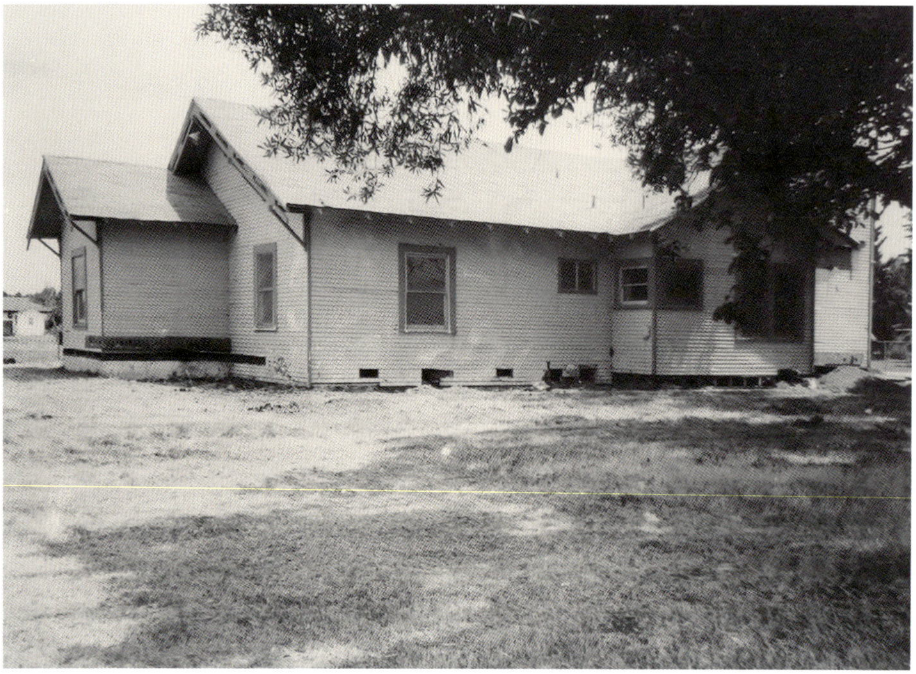

This home was in the country when it was built in 1917. At one point, the Ripon Dairy was located here. When the home was lifted to be moved, cow manure was still clinging to the floor joists. When the farm was no more, Peter and Anne Hekman purchased the home and raised a family there. But with the expansion of the downtown sector, Vermeulen & Co. purchased the property in 1995. Scott Dykstra bought the house and moved it to a new address on Oak Street. (Past image courtesy of Tom Vermeulen.)

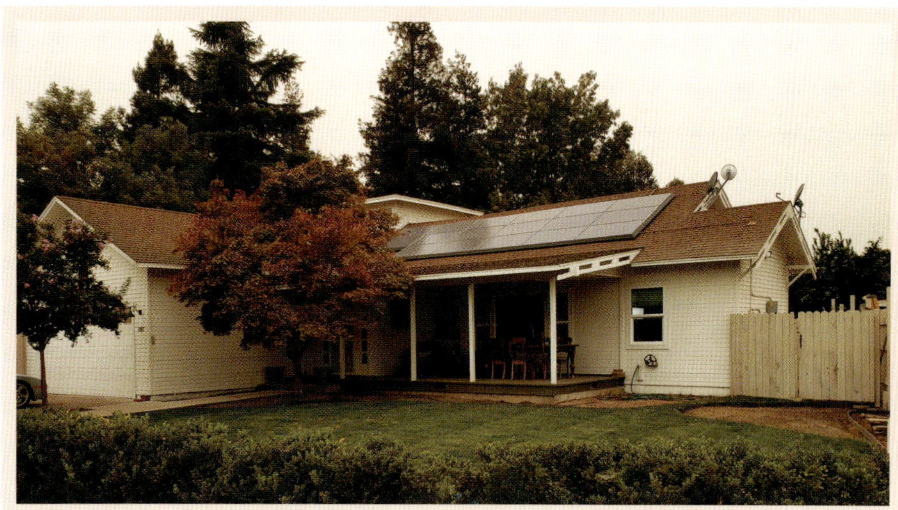

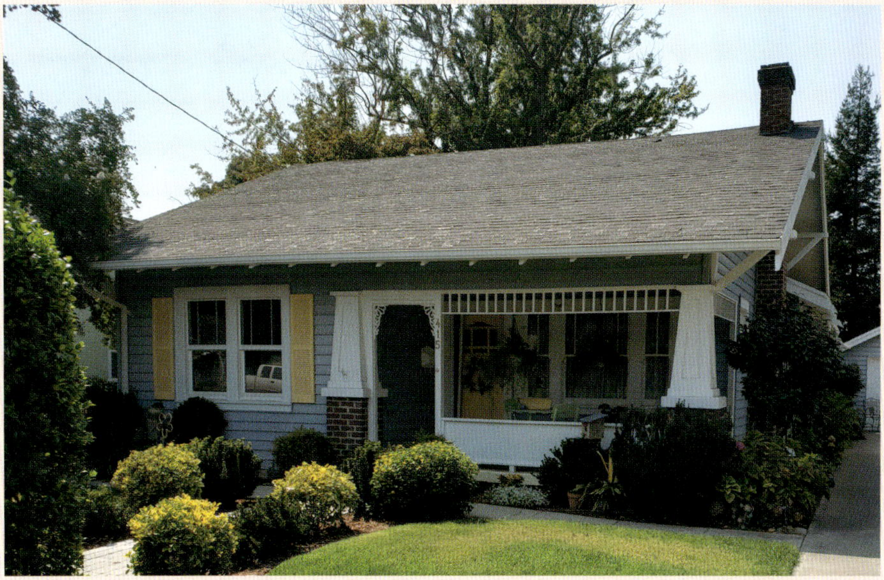

On February 1, 1921, the *Modesto Morning Herald* announced, "The building of a parsonage on Palm Avenue for the Swedish Bethany Mission Church is progressing rapidly. Most of the work is being done by members and friends of the church." The home stayed with the church until 1980, when Bill (a retired teacher) and Ann Betschart (a teacher) decided that city living sounded kind of nice. Bill wanted something new, and Ann wanted something old—from the look of things, Ann got her way. (Past image courtesy of the Betschart family.)

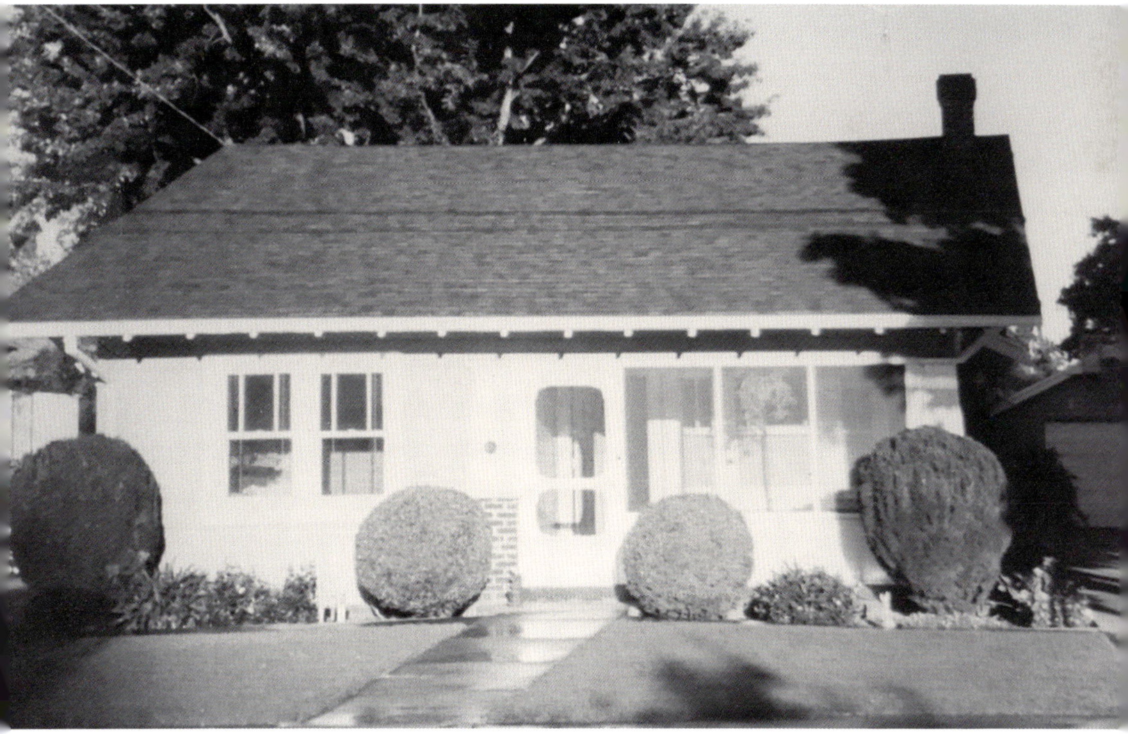

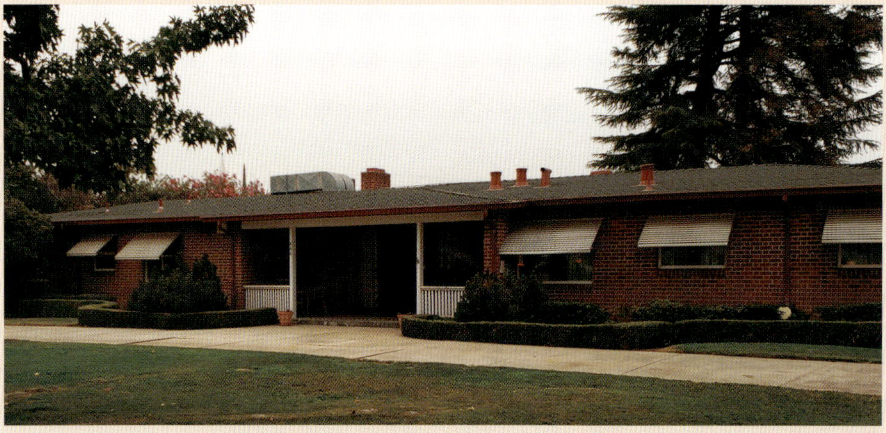

This home was built in 1948 by Keith Den Dulk, owner of the Den Dulk hardware store in Ripon. Dulk had built other homes in Ripon, and since he owned a hardware store, he decided to put all the latest gadgets into this grand house. In 1962, Bob and Aina Lange moved in, and the house came alive with entertainment and family. The pool in the backyard is a meeting place for the community. The Langes being in the restaurant business meant that guests would always get a good meal at their home. (Past image courtesy of Brenda Lange.)

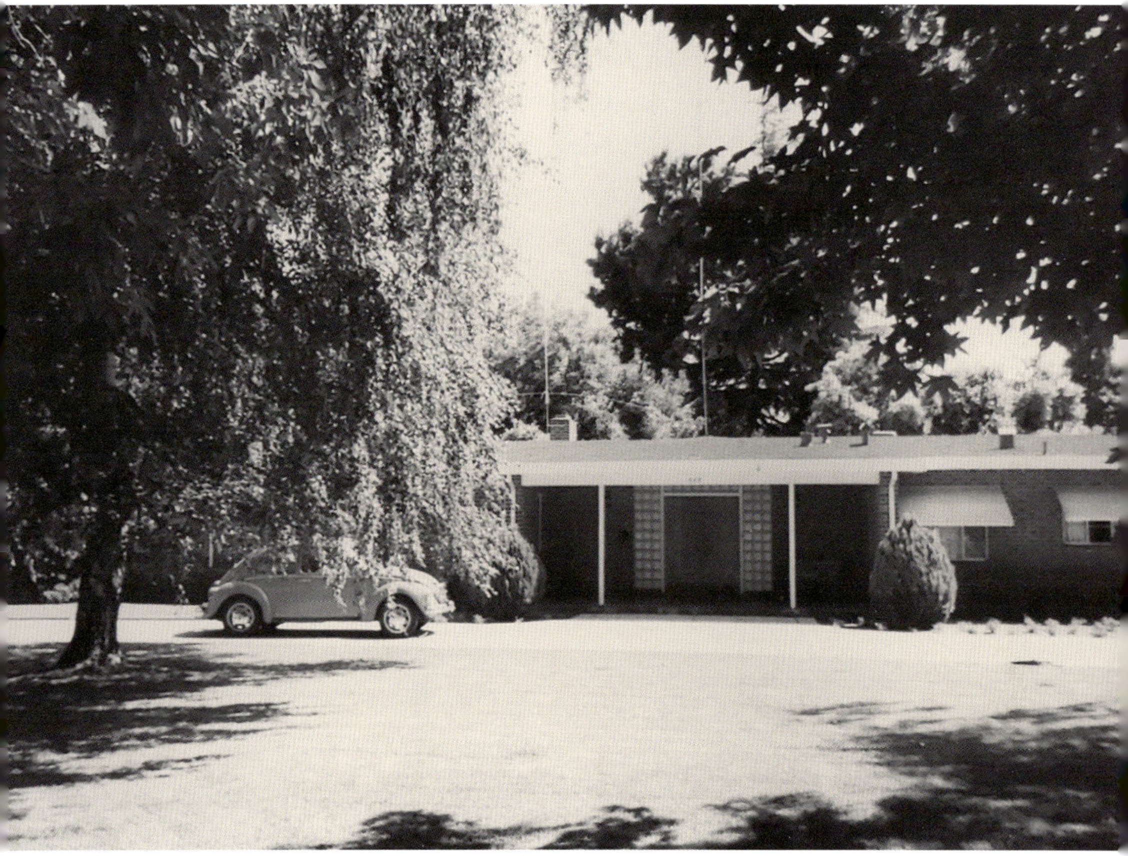

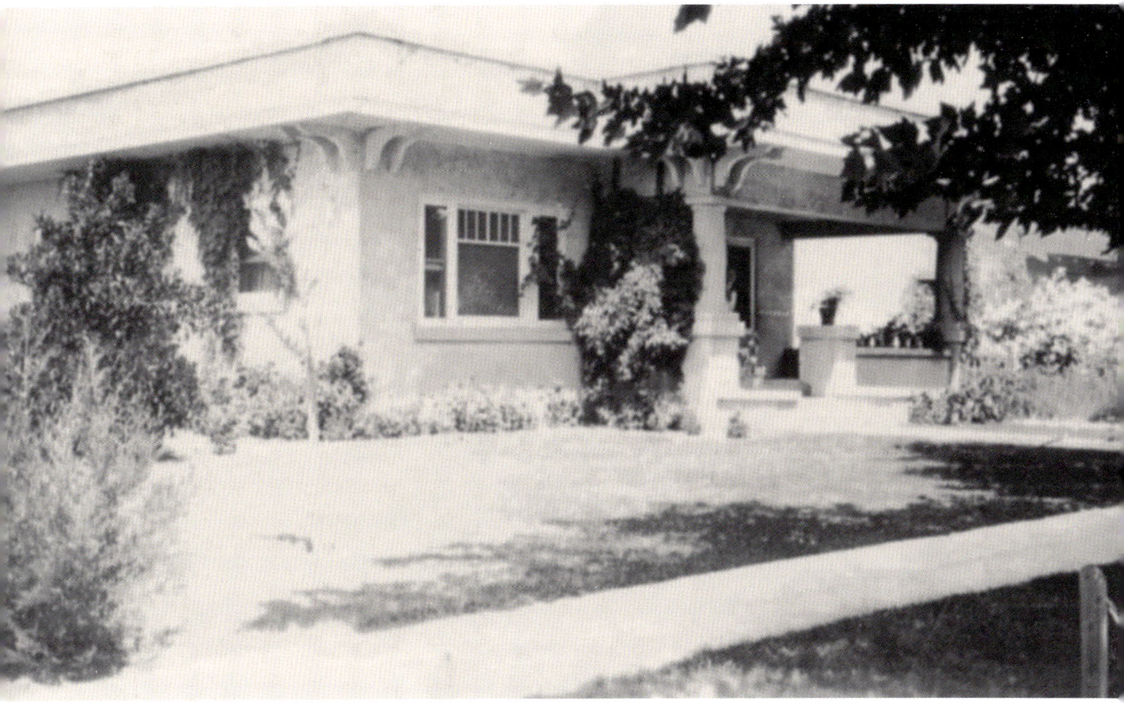

In 1921, Charles and Esther Turnquist of Alberta, Canada, moved to Ripon so they could open a hardware store. The home of Rev. Gustav Andrews, a former pastor of the Swedish church, was available, so they purchased it. In 1962, Clarence and Betty Smit took possession of this jewel. Clarence was the city administrator, so he looked after his home like he did the city—in a caring, gentle way. The home now has a new family to care for it: Paul and Kathleen Goulet. (Past image courtesy of the Goulet family.)

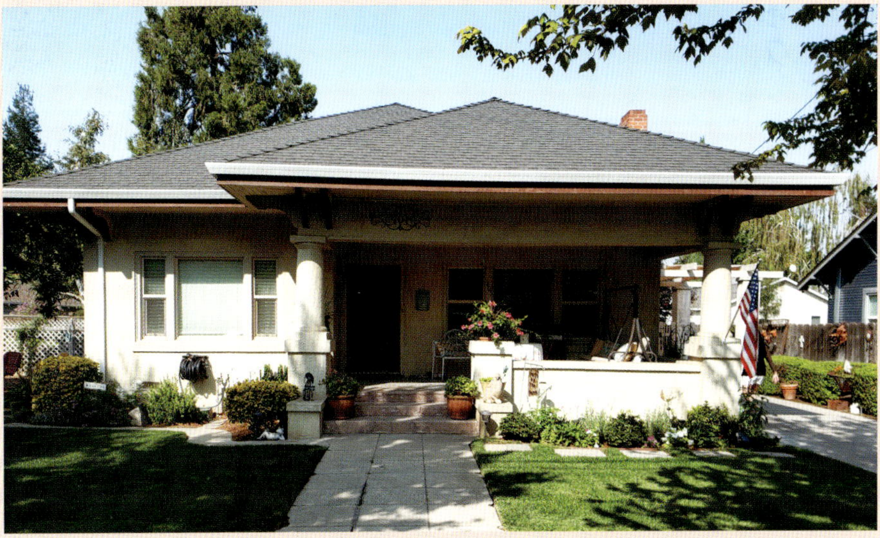

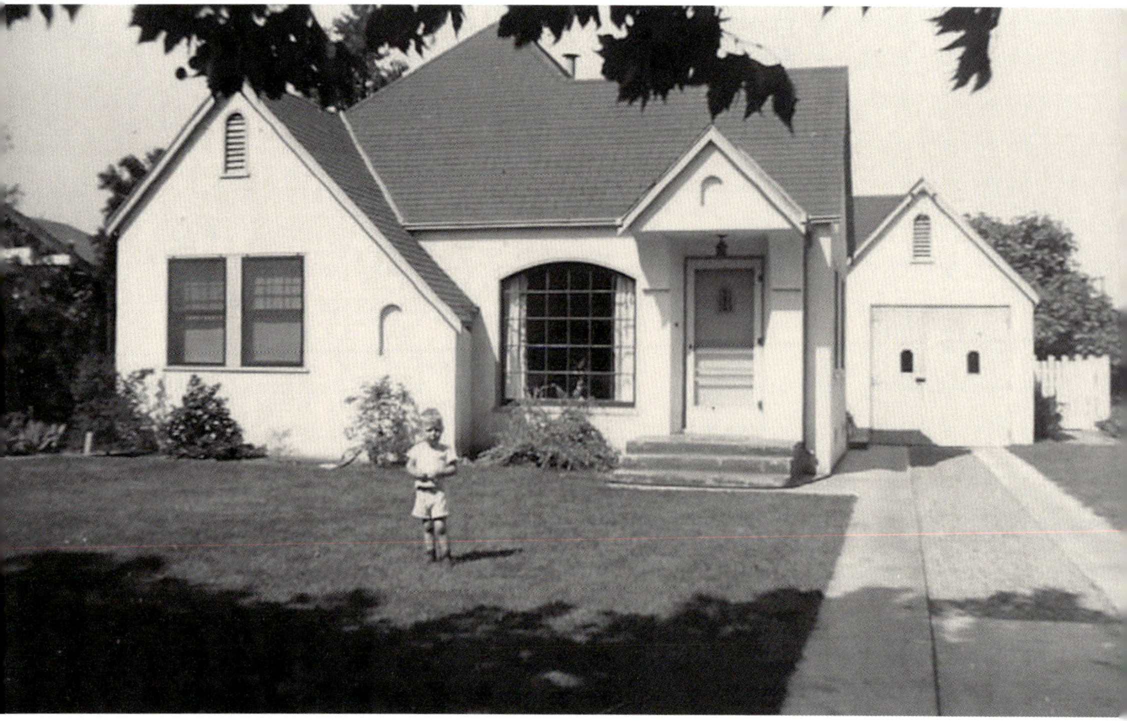

This could be called the home of music and giving. Allen and Fern Bugbee spent more than 50 years in this quaint cottage. Allen was involved in many community organizations. Fern was a teacher and loved music; one of the many instruments she was skilled with was the violin, which she played in the Modesto Symphony Orchestra. Allen supported whatever she did in music. After the couple's passing, they endowed the local American Legion with the majority of their estate.

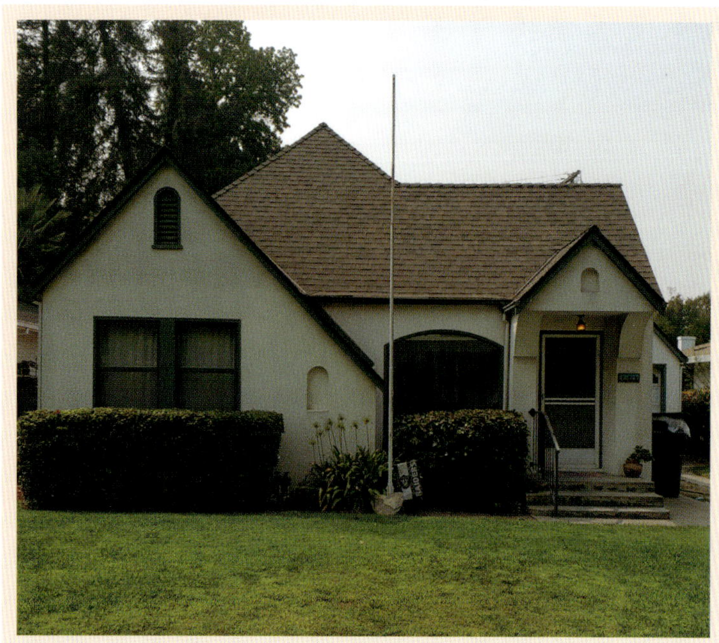

CHAPTER 3

Churches, the Heart of the Community

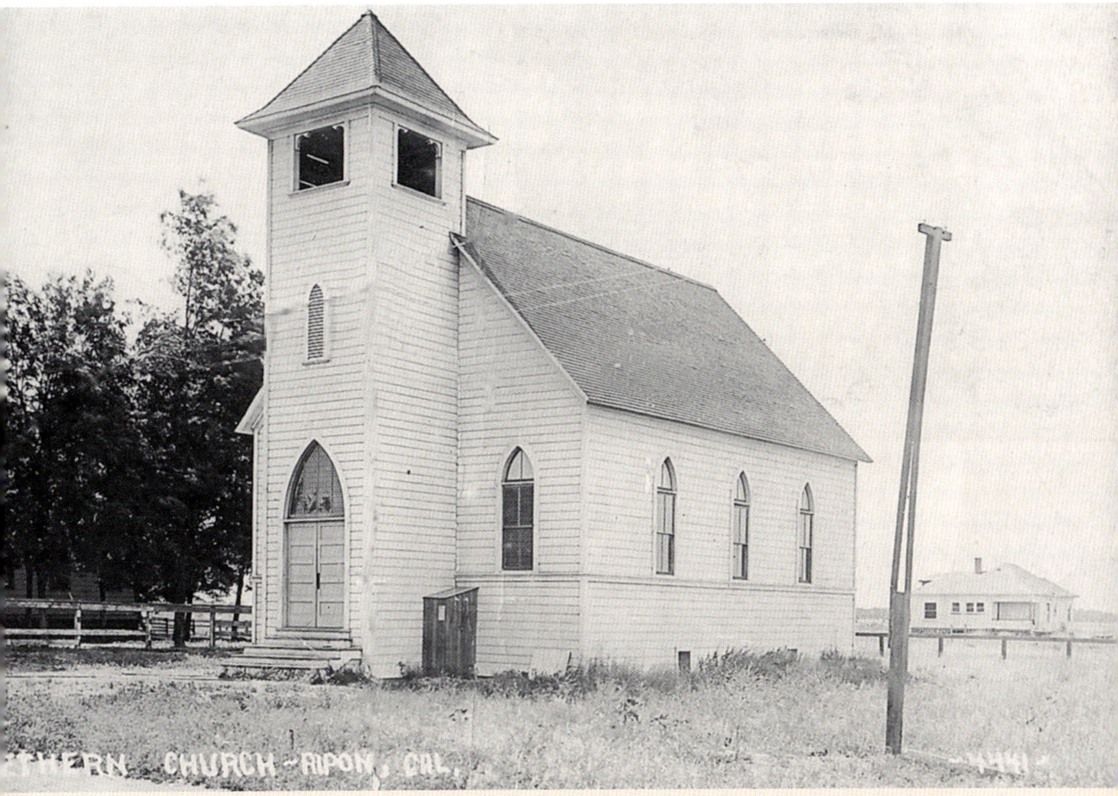

The heart of the community is its religious heritage; these ideas have made Ripon what it is today. These deeply rooted values have played an integral part in making these churches the heart of Ripon. In 1884, the Women's Improvement Club decided that Ripon needed a house of worship, and these fine ladies were the turning point to give this community what it was needing.

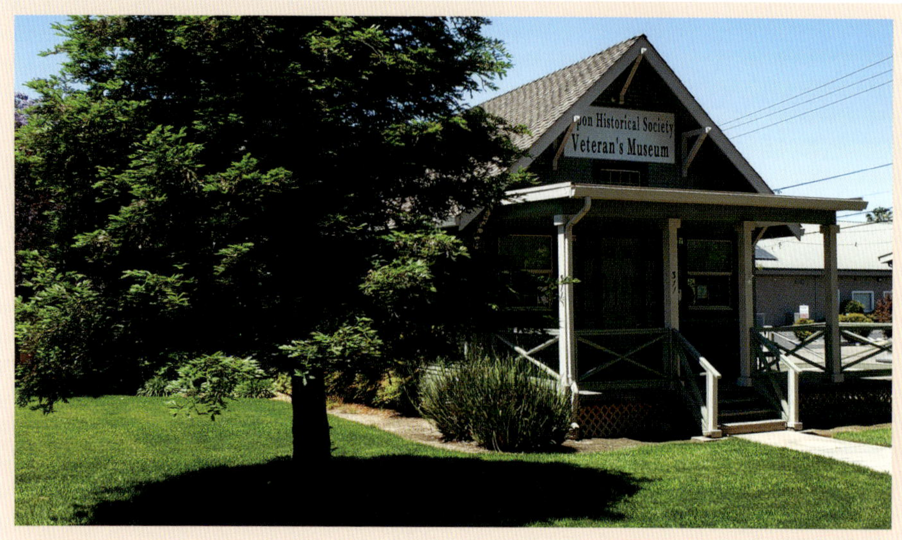

In 1911, the dream of a Christian Reformed Church in Ripon was developing. L.P. Brink, F. Stuart, and J. Vissia made it happen, and the Society for the Promotion of the Spiritual Welfare of Hollanders at Ripon was formed. The pristine church was dedicated in 1917, and the principals decided to call it First Christian Reformed Church of Ripon—a simpler name. On February 4, 1918, twenty-nine individuals became the charter members of the church.

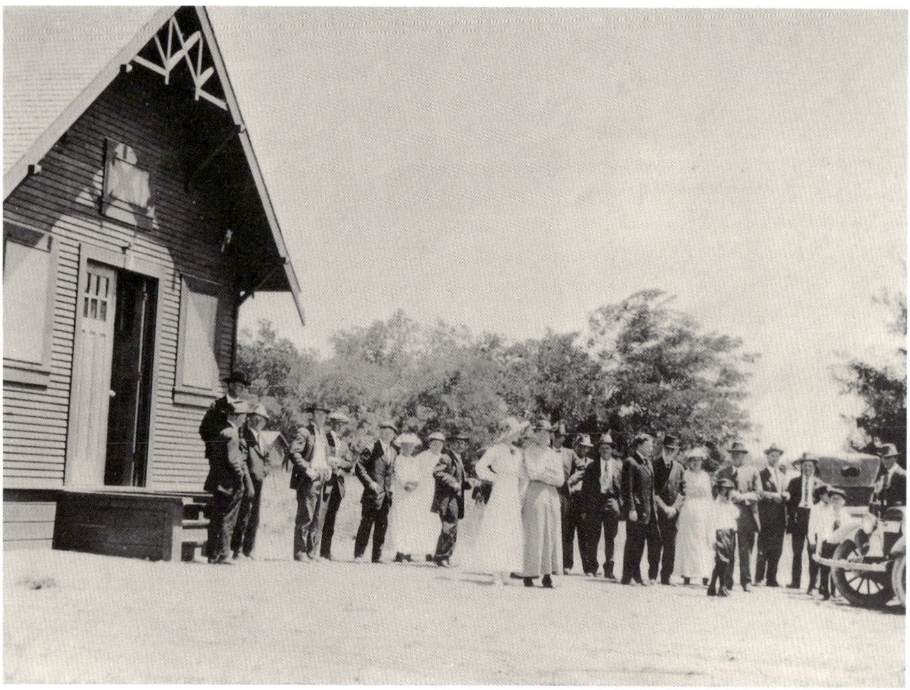

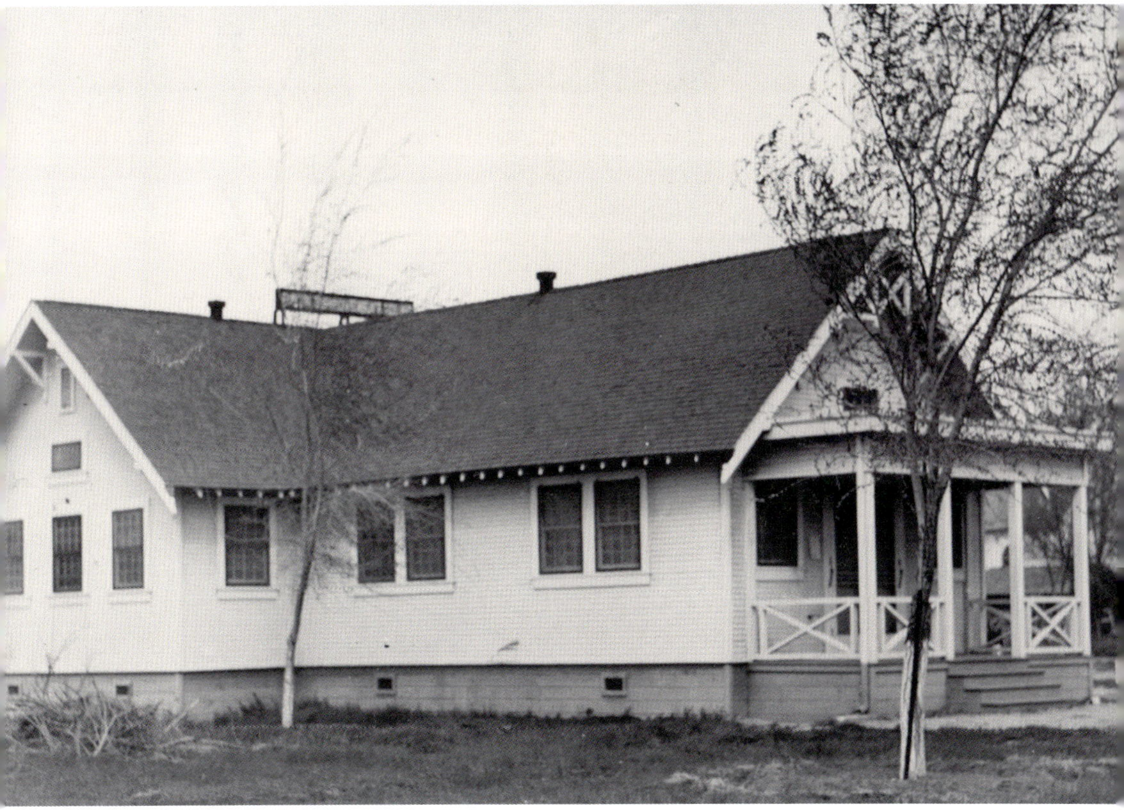

The First Christian Reformed Church served the congregation well until the growing church needed more spacious quarters. On May 3, 1924, the cornerstone was laid for a new church, which was not empty for very long. The Women's Improvement Club, the organization that started the first house of worship in Ripon in 1884, bought the building and began using it for weddings and baptisms and other social functions. When the chamber of commerce formed, the Women's Improvement Club allowed the chamber to use the building as an office.

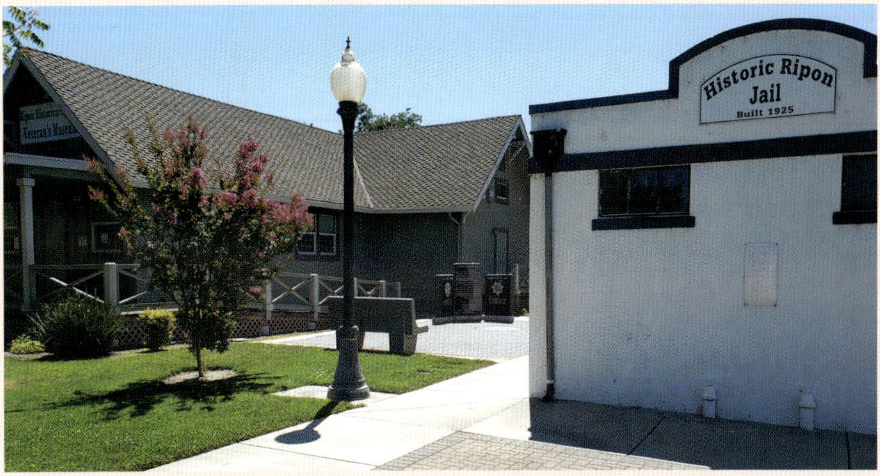

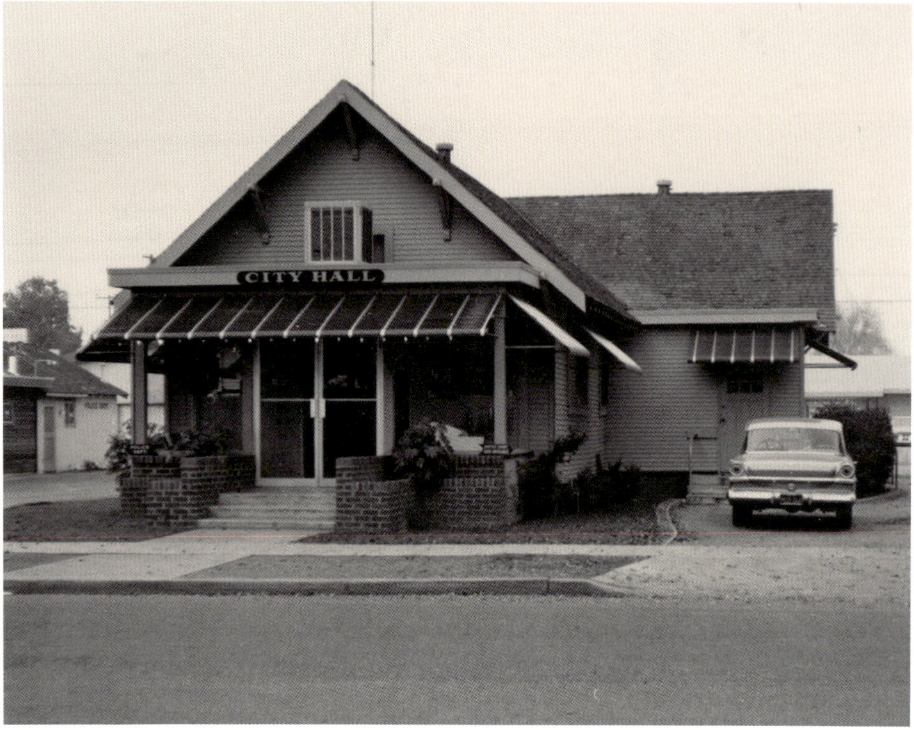

In 1945, when the city was incorporated, First Christian Reformed Church was used as a city hall. When the city hall moved to new quarters, this building sat vacant for a short period. The author of this book, along with some other individuals, persuaded the city to make the building a veterans' museum, which it now is.

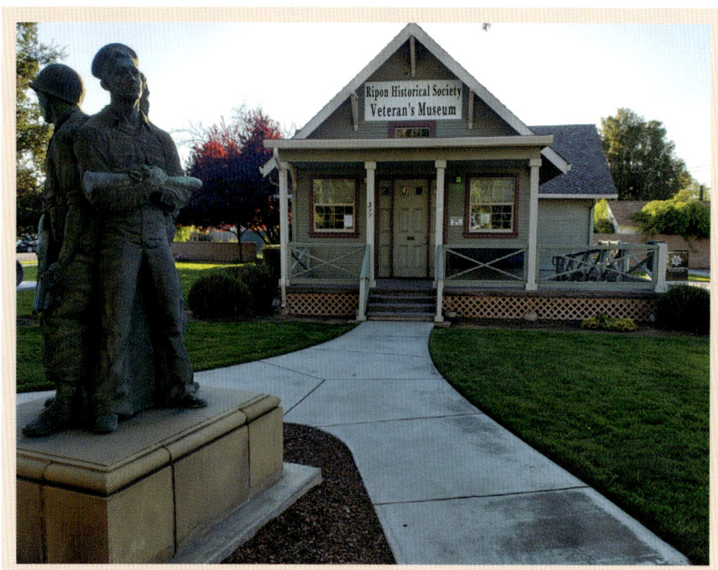

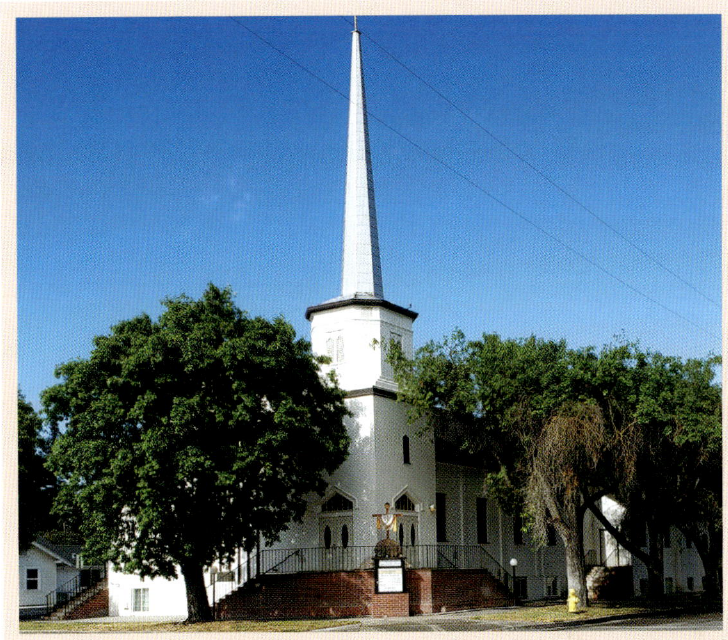

On August 21, 1924, the new First Christian Reformed Church was dedicated on the corner of Orange Avenue and Second Street with a crowd of 400 listening to Rev. John DeJong serving as master of ceremonies. With the church's grand edifice and a spacious basement for receptions, the congregation felt they had done well. The congregation needed more room in 1987, so the planning committee started looking for a new site. A new church was dedicated on May 18, 2003. The church building on Orange Avenue was sold to St. Mark Coptic Orthodox Church.

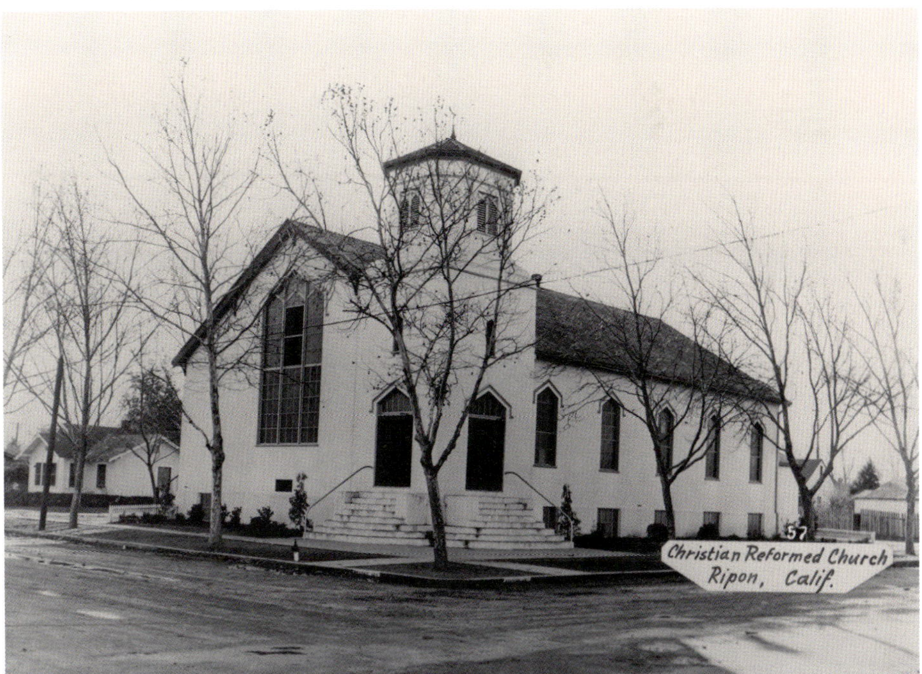

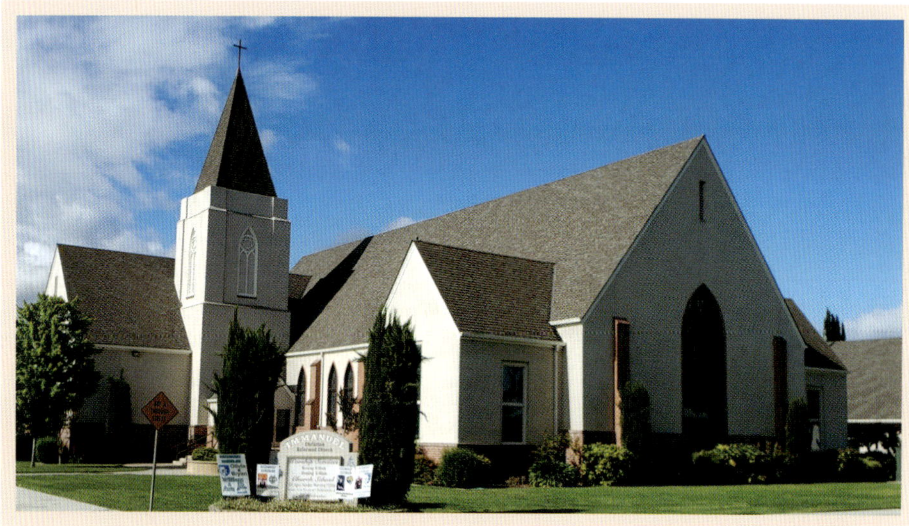

After World War II, First Christian Reformed Church was brimming with worshippers, and it was apparent that a new congregation was needed. So, 45 families and 5 individuals became a new church on March 11, 1946, when Immanuel Christian Reformed Church of Ripon was organized. The first service was held in the building erected for the First Christian Reformed Church in 1917, which was too small. Finally, on February 29, 1952, after six years of temporary homes, a new church building was dedicated.

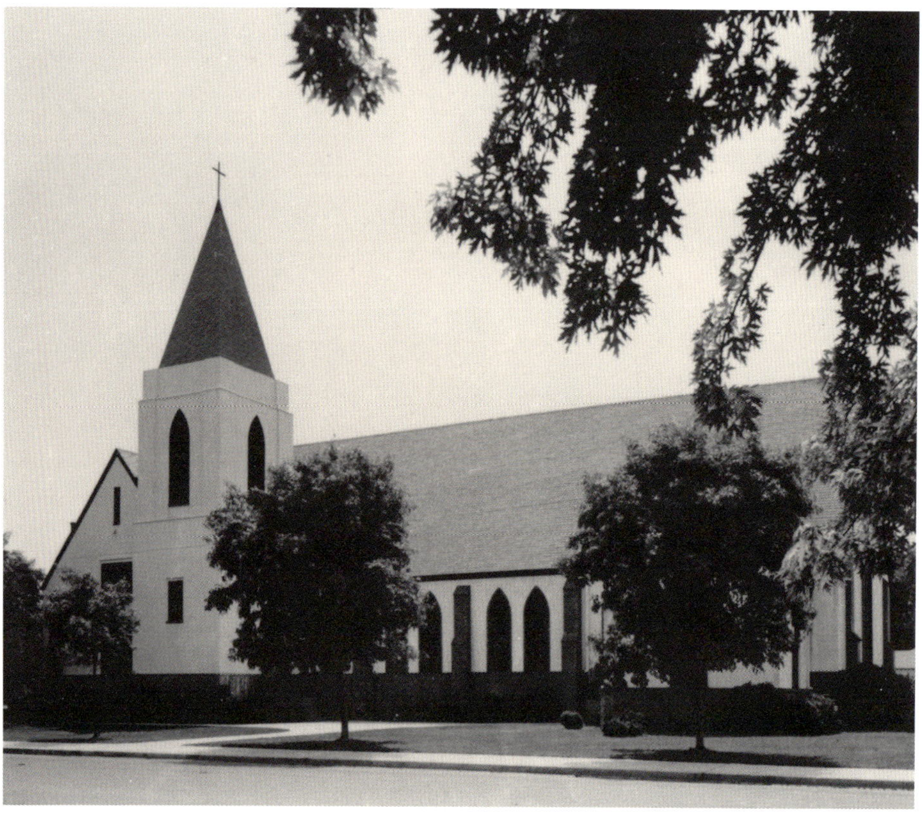

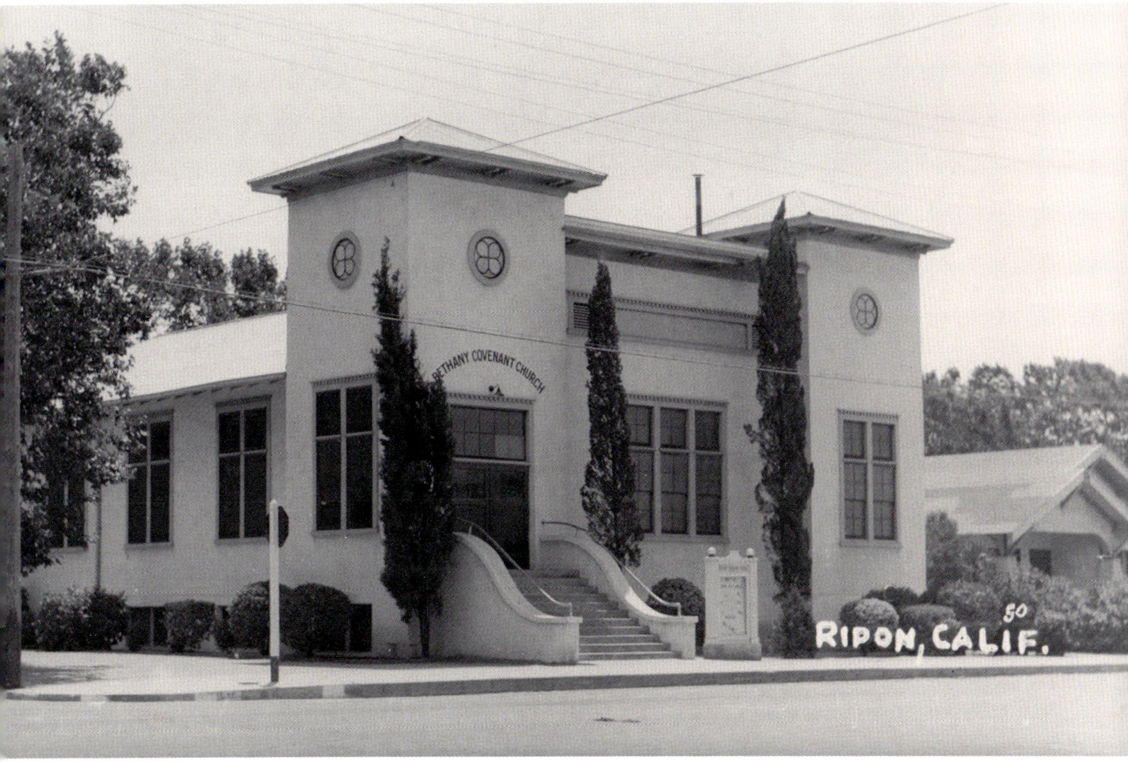

The Swedish Mission Church was organized in the home of J. Emanuel Johnson on January 21, 1916. A gift from Mr. and Mrs. Claus Lindblom made it possible to erect a new church building for $10,000. The church was dedicated in 1920. In the 1930s, the Swedish language was still being used there, but the church began to see the need for a language transition. It was decided on January 1, 1941, that English would be used, and the name would be changed to Bethany Covenant Church. In 2003, Bethany Covenant Church changed its name to Heartland Community Church.

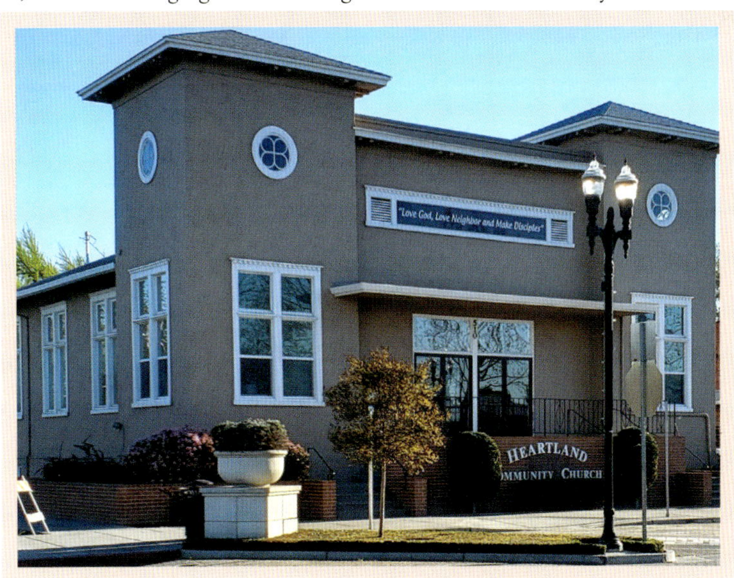

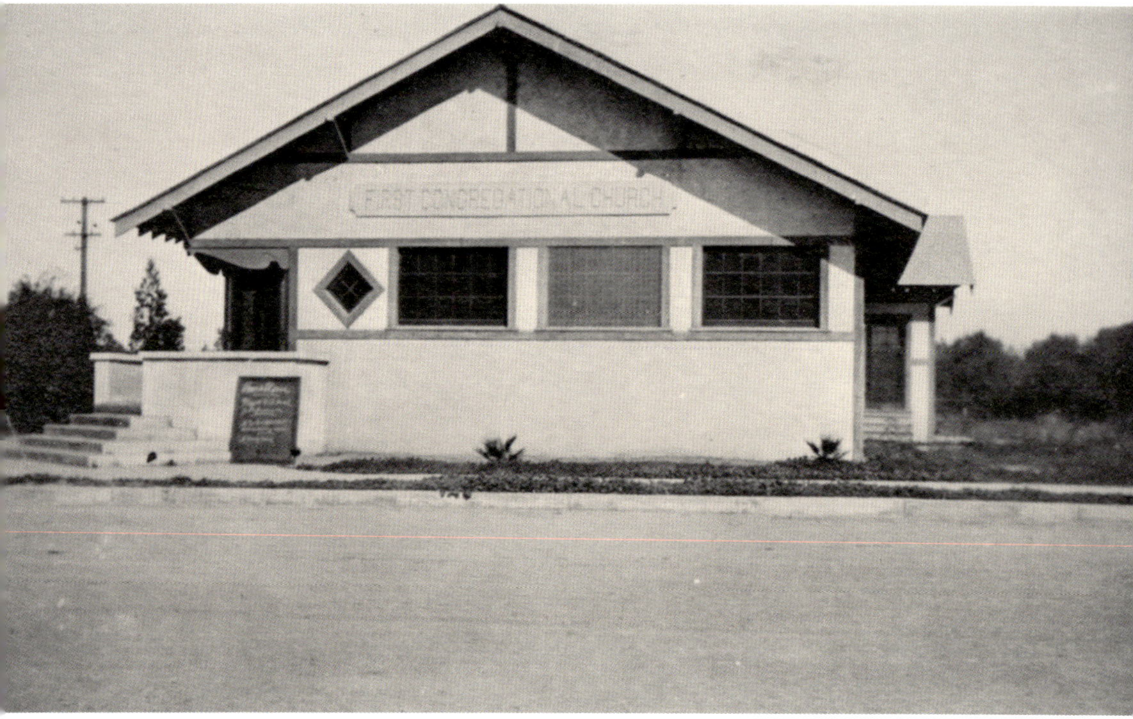

On May 20, 1917, the First Congregational Church was dedicated by Rev. J.J. Kelly. It was clear on the date of the dedication that funds had run $475 short. Rev. L.D. Rathbone of Berkeley, who preached the dedicatory sermon, asked the 200 people assembled for pledges to allow the project to be concluded free of debt. Within 10 minutes, $425 was pledged, and the remaining $50 soon followed. The building has changed little over the 100-odd years, and the congregation is still healthy.

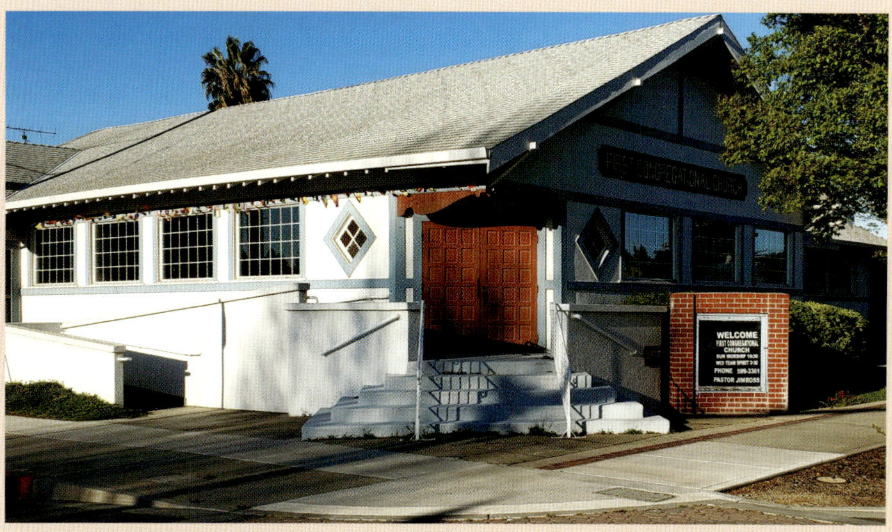

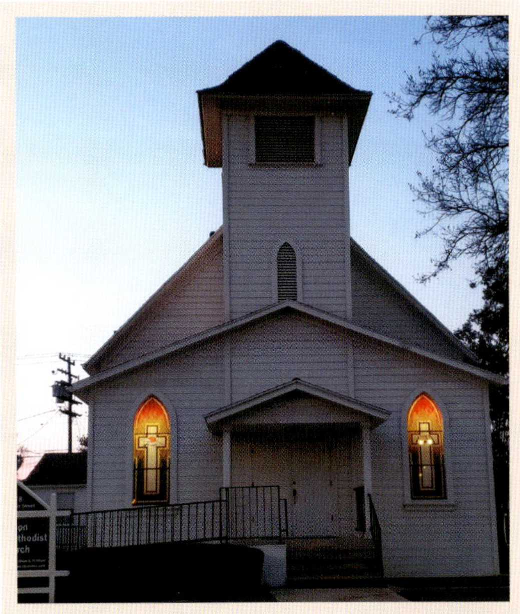

In 1884, the members of the Women's Improvement Club, first organized to care for Ripon's cemetery, turned their attention to the construction of a church that could be used by several denominations. Until that point, services had been held in private homes, outdoors, or in tents. After the building was completed, different denominations used the structure for years. After all denominations had erected buildings of their own, the church sat unused for years. In 1929, the Methodists purchased the abandoned church for $900, breathing new life into the house of worship.

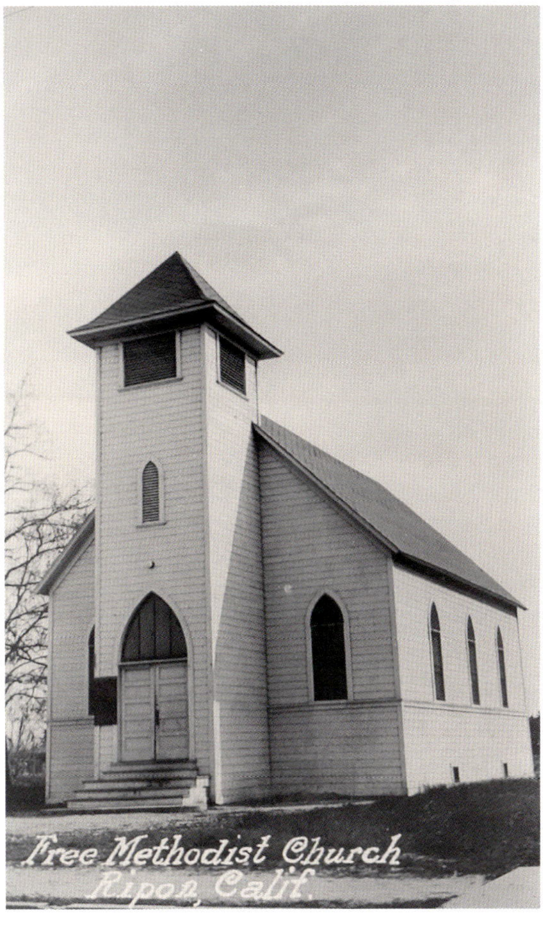

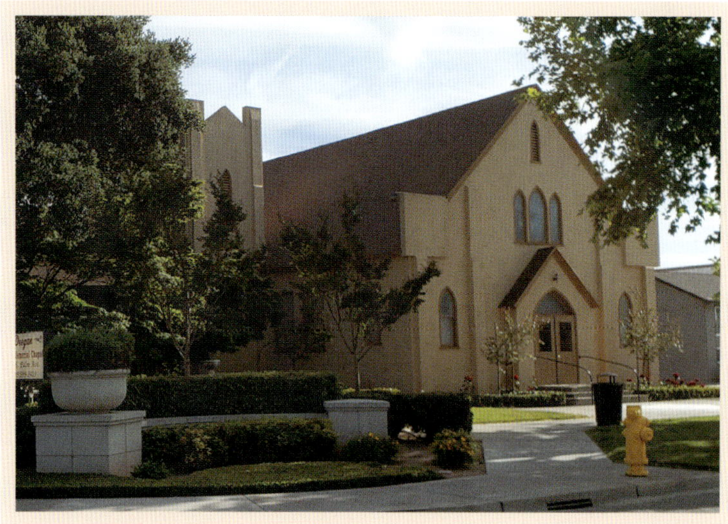

On August 27, 1934, Calvary Reformed Church was organized in the home of Derk Van Konynenburg Sr. The first services took place on September 7, 1934, in the American Legion Hall. It was decided in January 1937 that two lots on the corner of Main and Palm Streets would be purchased for a church. The church cost $7,400 to build and was dedicated on April 6, 1937. On September 27, 1948, the congregation purchased property at the corner of Second Street and Vera Avenue. The old church was sold to James J. Kroll and became the Ripon Mortuary, which opened on February 26, 1949.

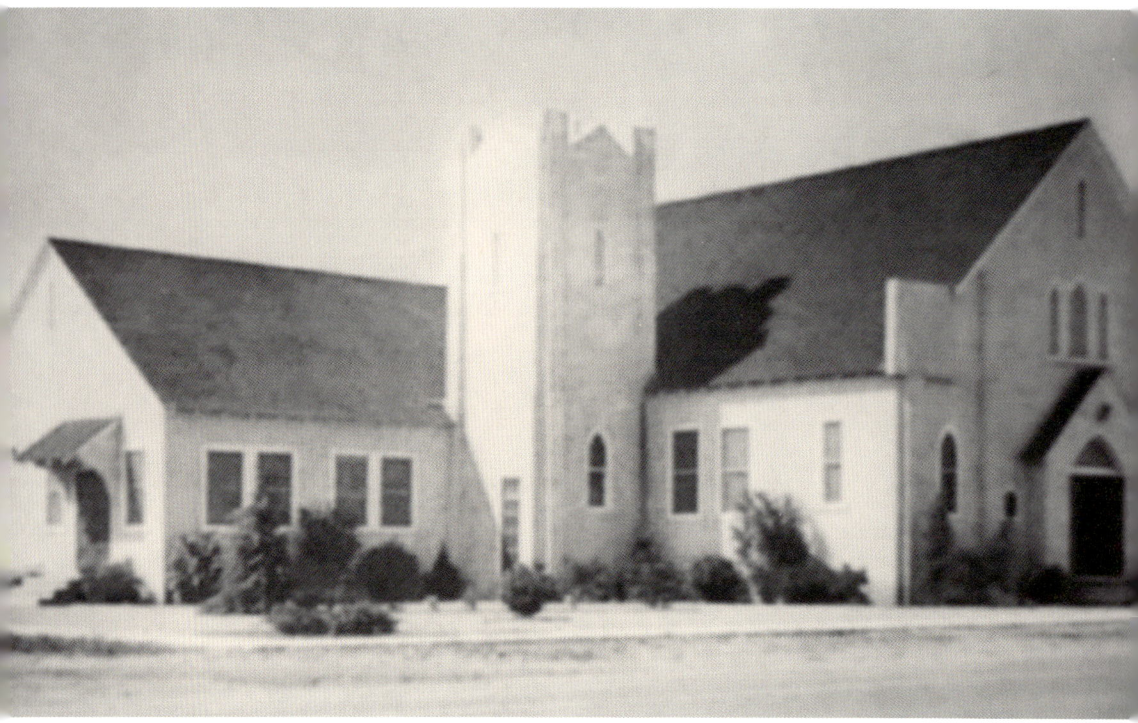

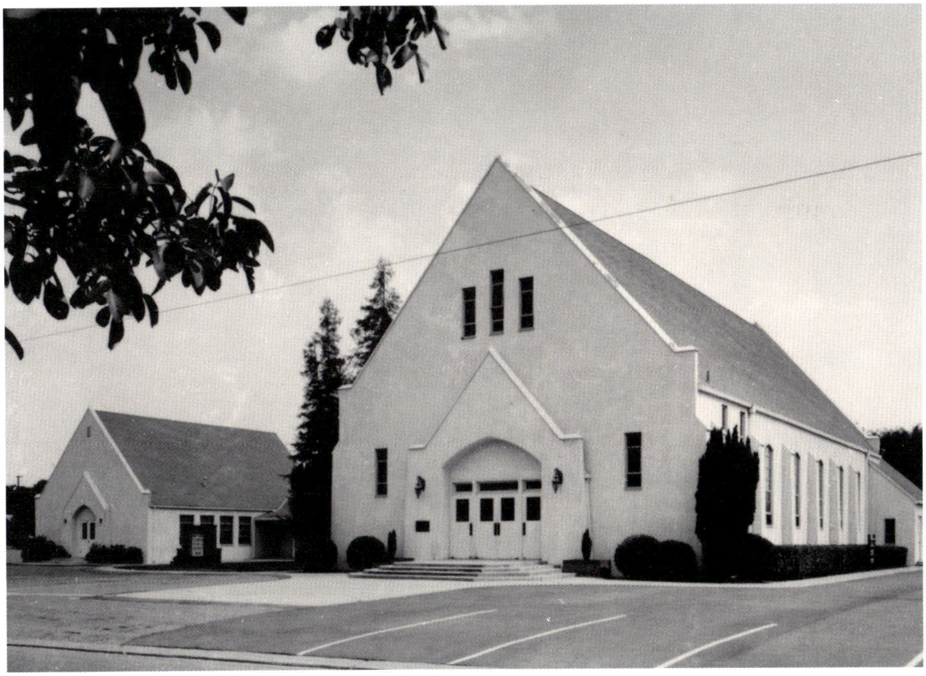

On September 27, 1948, with the singing of "How Firm a Foundation," Reverend Keuning moved the first shovel of dirt for the new Calvary Reformed Church. From that point on, Henry Beuving, the builder, worked tirelessly to get the church ready for its dedication on July 4, 1949. The $100,000 church was equipped with two manual Wurlitzer organs to serve the 125 families that were part of the congregation.

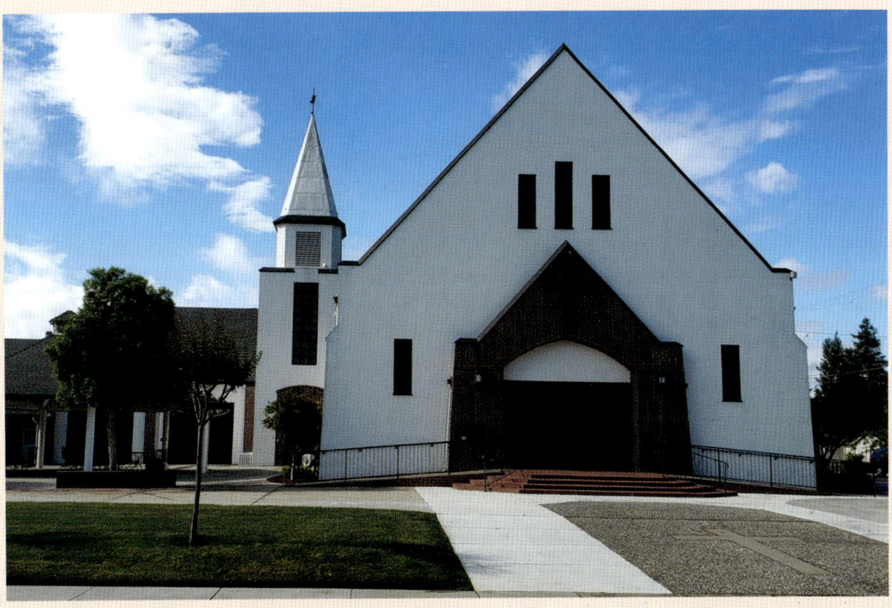

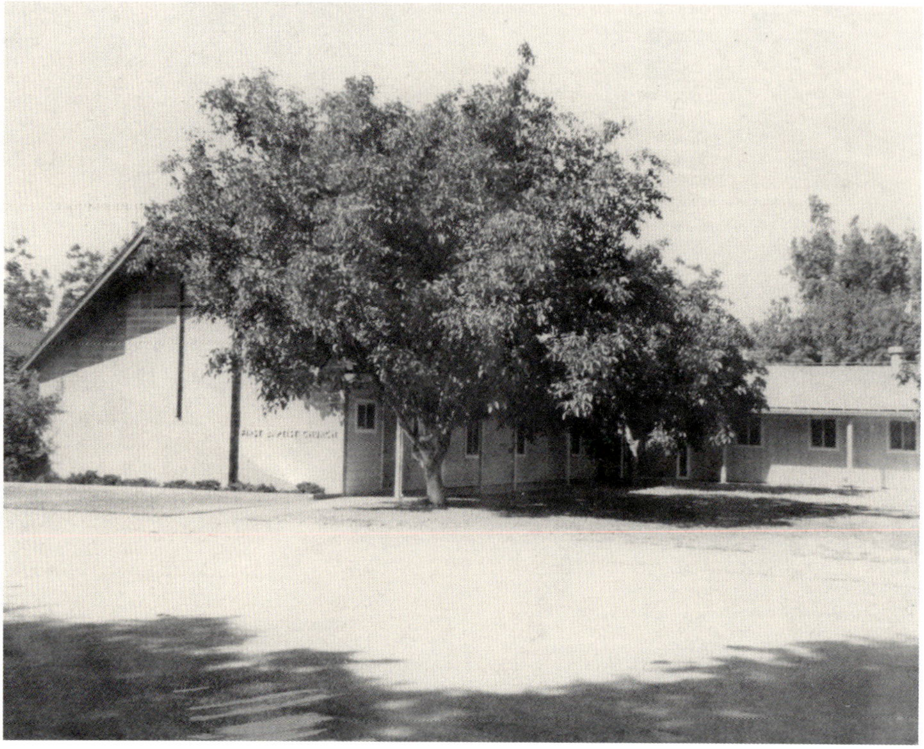

The Odd Fellows Hall played host to many new churches throughout the years. On February 29, 1948, the First Baptist Church was founded. Within the first few months, it was decided that a more spacious location was needed, so a dirt lot was rented on North Stockton Avenue. The church started in a tent on October 15, 1948. The congregation was growing, and it took time to find a lot on which to build a church. Two lots near the corner of Milgeo and Ripona Avenues were purchased for $700, and in 1951, the building was completed.

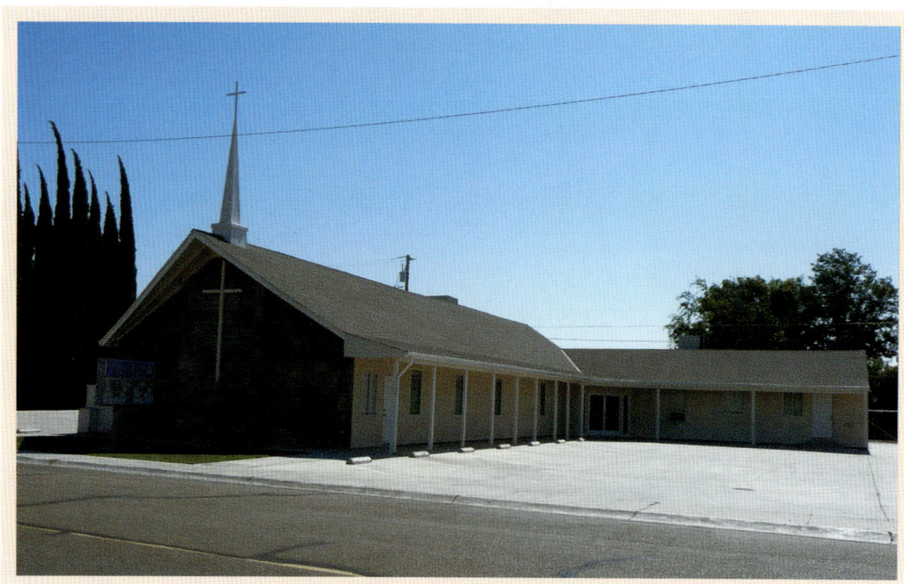

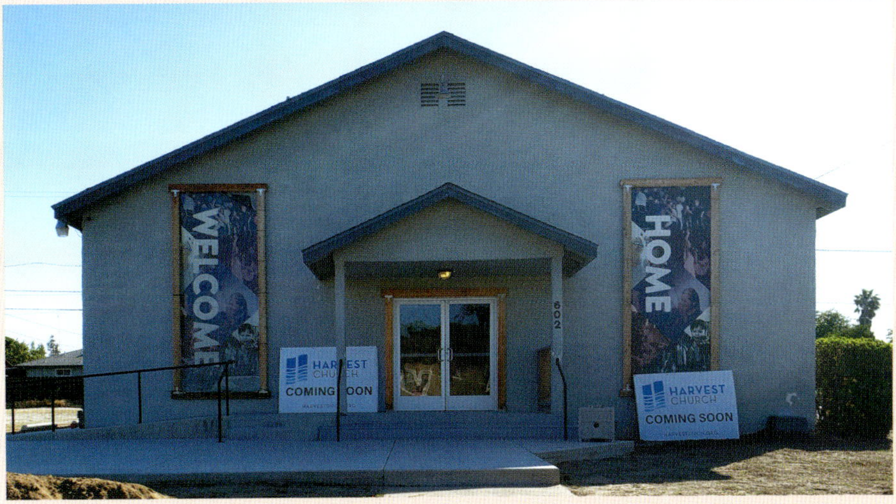

On December 4, 1944, the Good Tidings Church of the Assemblies of God was started in the Odd Fellows Hall. By 1950, the congregation had a church at the corner of 602 Ripona Avenue. It had many name changes. In February 2016, it became One Church under the Assembly of God; like so many of the churches with growing numbers of congregants, it soon needed new quarters, so it moved to a new space in August 2019. Now this understated building will serve a new congregation, Harvest Church.

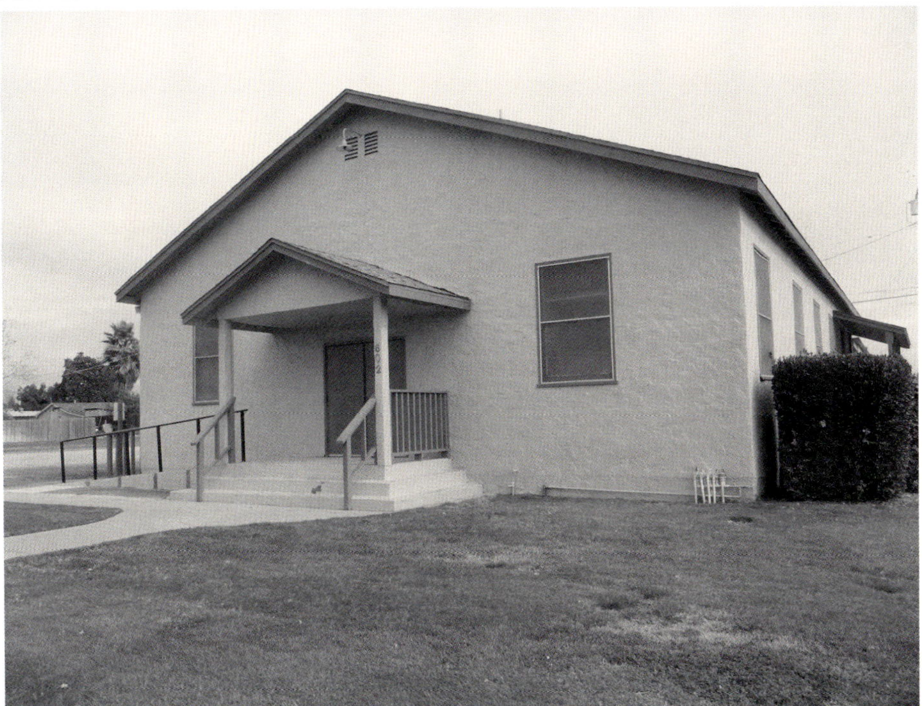

Consistent with our mission to preserve history on a local level, this book was printed in South Carolina on American-made paper and manufactured entirely in the United States. Products carrying the accredited Forest Stewardship Council (FSC) label are printed on 100 percent FSC-certified paper.

MADE IN THE USA